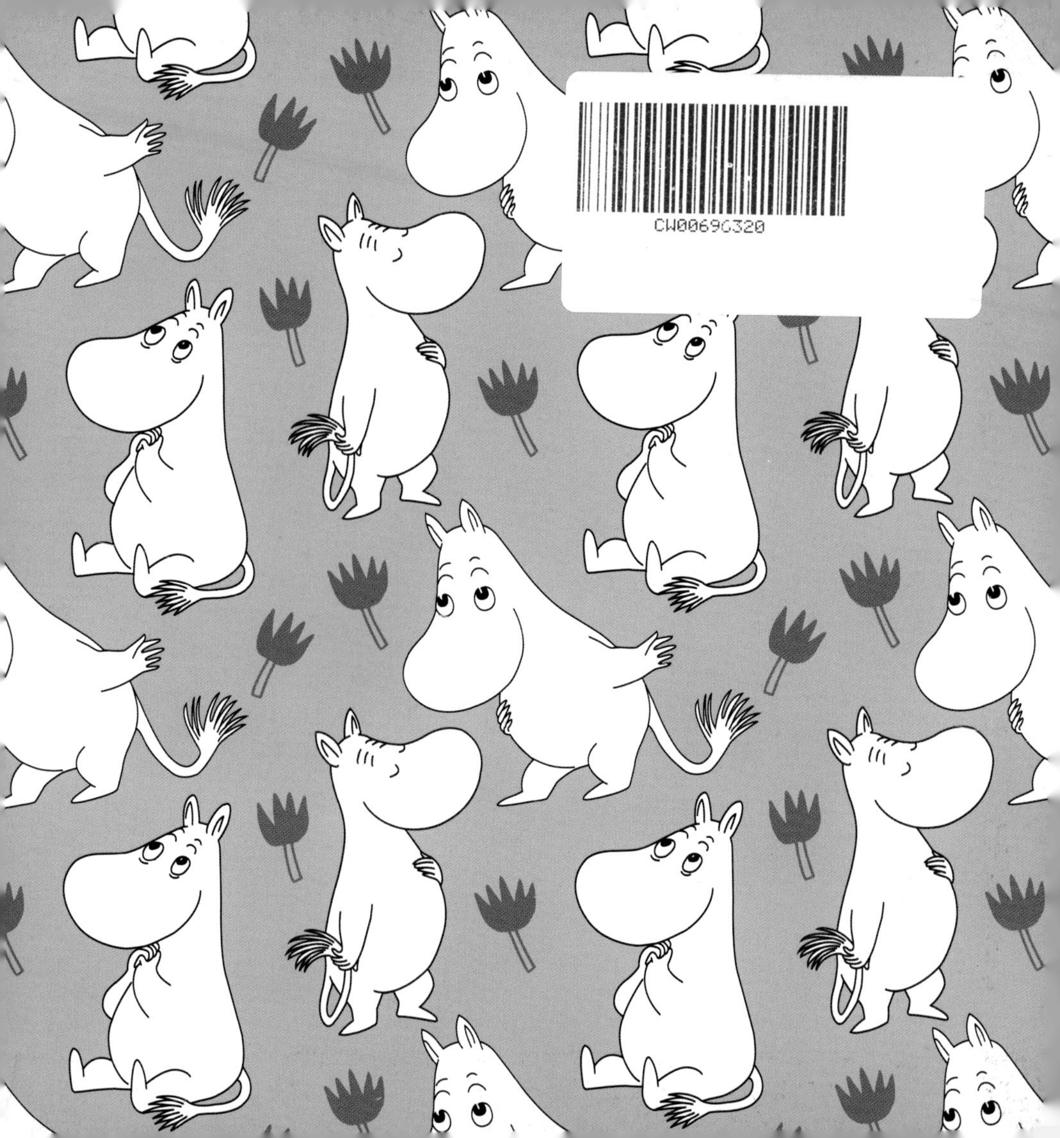

Published by Ice House Books

© 2019 Moomin Characters™

Edited by Samantha Rigby
Designed by Richard Peck
Photography credits page 61

Ice House Books is an imprint of Half Moon Bay Limited
The Ice House, 124 Walcot Street, Bath, BA1 5BG
www.halfmoonbay.co.uk

ISBN 978-1-912867-00-4

Printed in China

MOOMIN®
COMFORT FOOD

ICE HOUSE BOOKS

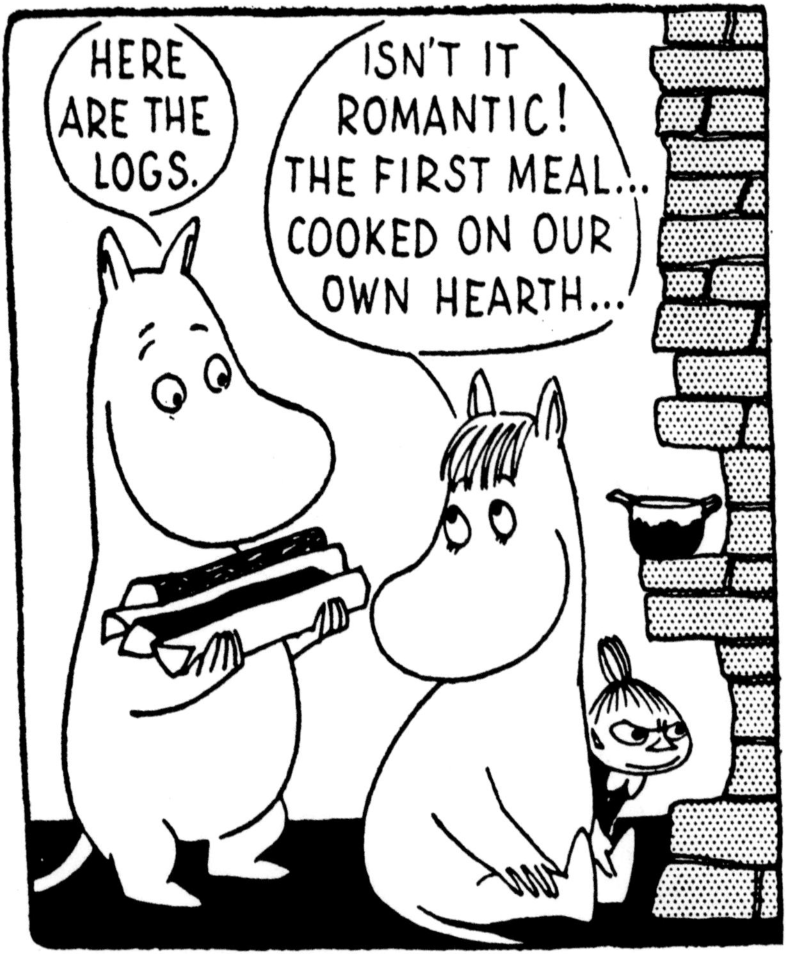
HERE ARE THE LOGS.
ISN'T IT ROMANTIC! THE FIRST MEAL... COOKED ON OUR OWN HEARTH...

CONTENTS

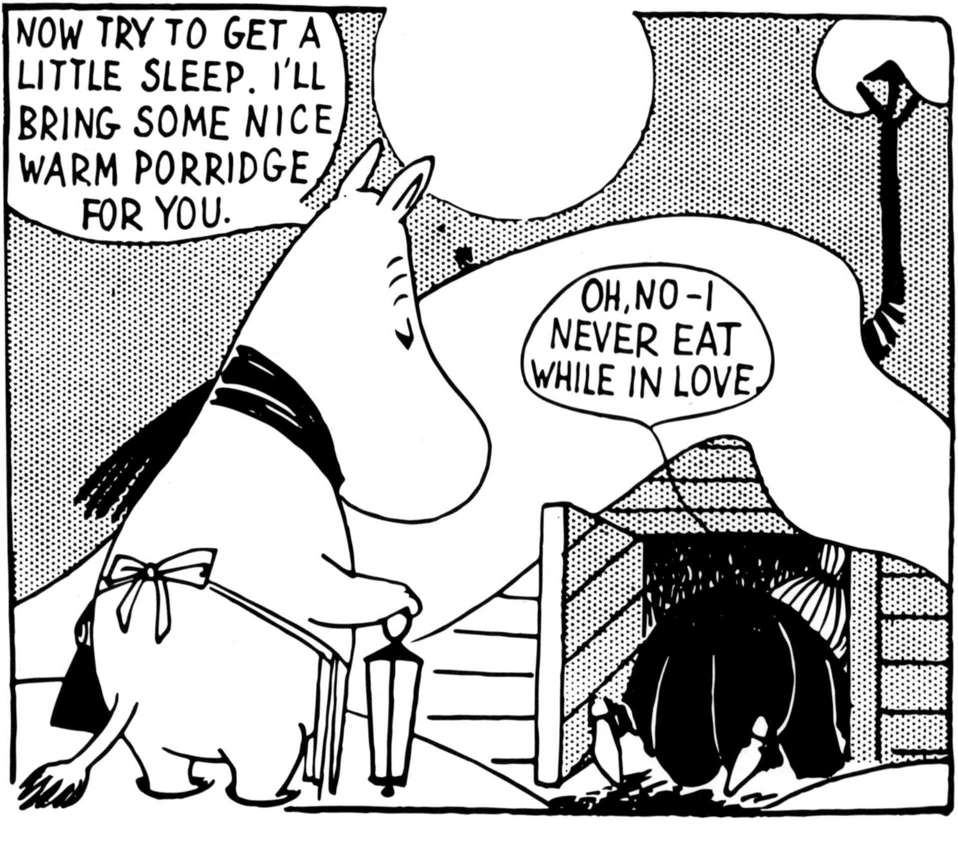
NOW TRY TO GET A LITTLE SLEEP. I'LL BRING SOME NICE WARM PORRIDGE FOR YOU.
OH, NO - I NEVER EAT WHILE IN LOVE.

NICE WARM
PORRIDGE

Ingredients

20g rolled oats
180ml milk (or alternative)
pinch of ground cinnamon
pinch of sea salt
1 handful fresh blueberries
1 tsp unsweetened coconut flakes
a few pumpkin seeds

Makes: 1 bowl
Cook time: 10 minutes

Method

1. Place the rolled oats, milk, cinnamon and salt into a saucepan and bring to a gentle simmer.

2. Continue to simmer for around 5 minutes, until the oats are softened, then transfer into a bowl.

3. Scatter the blueberries, pumpkin seeds and coconut flakes on top of your porridge – and enjoy!

Porridge is so good for your digestion!

VERY GOOD
PANCAKES

Ingredients

250ml milk (or alternative)
1 large free-range egg
2 tbsp vegetable oil
125g all-purpose flour
2 tsp baking powder
2 tbsp sugar
1 pinch of salt
fresh berries & maple syrup (topping)

Makes: 10 pancakes
Prep time: 5 minutes
Cook time: 15 minutes

Method

1. Place a heat-proof plate in the oven and heat it to 90°C/200°F – ready to keep your cooked pancakes warm.

2. Put the flour, sugar, baking powder and salt in a bowl and mix well. Set aside.

3. Put the milk, vegetable oil and egg in a separate bowl and whisk together.

4. Pour the dry mixture into the liquid mixture and stir to combine (don't over-mix).

5. Heat a frying pan over a medium heat and coat with vegetable oil. Spoon a dollop of batter on to the pan and allow to spread out slightly. Cook until the surface has a few bubbles (about 1 minute). Then flip carefully with a spatula and cook until brown on the underside (1 or 2 minutes more).

6. Transfer each cooked pancake to the plate in the oven and cover with foil until you're ready to eat.

7. Serve warm, with maple syrup and fresh berries on top!

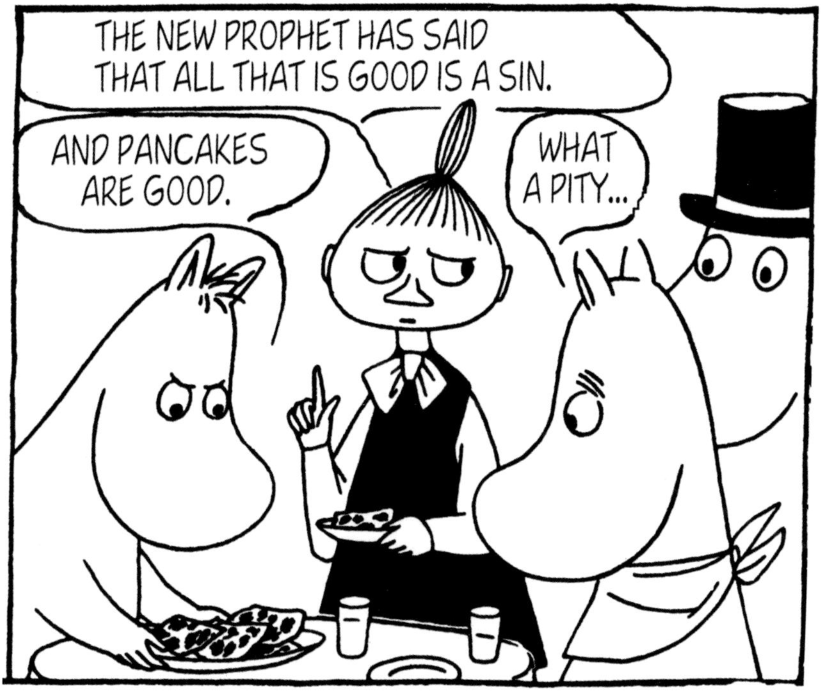
THE NEW PROPHET HAS SAID THAT ALL THAT IS GOOD IS A SIN.
AND PANCAKES ARE GOOD.
WHAT A PITY...

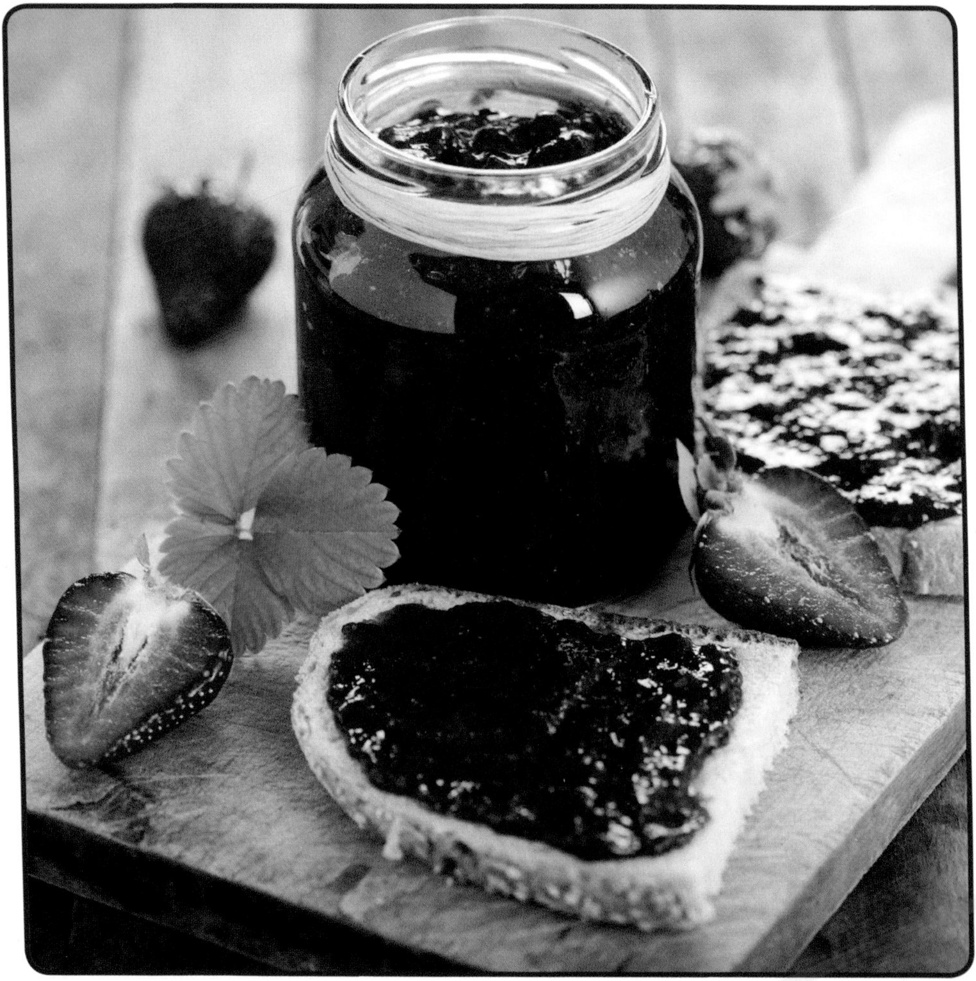

MOOMINMAMMA'S

STRAWBERRY JAM

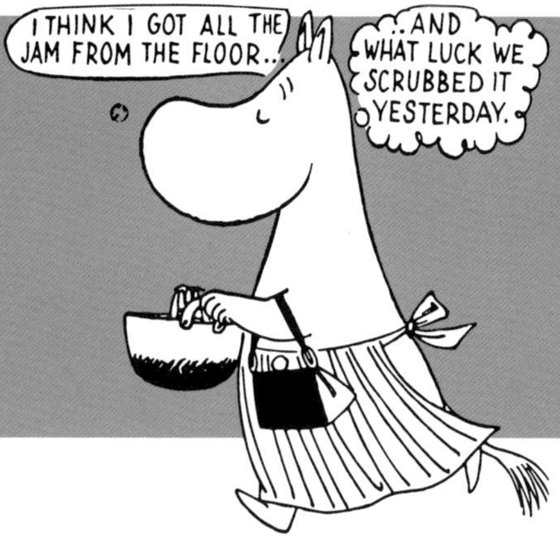
I THINK I GOT ALL THE JAM FROM THE FLOOR...
...AND WHAT LUCK WE SCRUBBED IT YESTERDAY.

Ingredients

680g strawberries
2 tbsp apple juice
1 tbsp lemon juice

Makes: 6 jars (approx.)
Prep time: 20 minutes
Cook time: 20 minutes
Extra time: 12 hours cooling

Method

1. First, sterilise your jars. Heat the oven to 120°C/250°F. Place your clean jars on a baking tray with space in between them. Put them in the oven for 20 minutes then turn off the heat, but leave the jars in the oven until your jam is ready – you should always put warm jam into warm jars.

2. Wash your strawberries, remove the stems and chop them into quarters. Place them into a large saucepan, add the apple and lemon juices and mix until well combined.

3. Simmer the mixture over a low heat, stirring and squishing regularly with a wooden spoon, until the jam becomes thick and smooth. Ensure the jam doesn't stick to the bottom of the pan or burn, and if it seems too thick, add a small amount of cold water (but not too much).

4. Once the jam is thick and smooth, pour it into your sterilised jars and seal them. Allow to cool for 12 hours, then store in the fridge and enjoy within two weeks – on top of toast, pancakes or porridge!

WARMING
CARROT SOUP

Ingredients

3 tbsp olive oil, plus extra for serving
2 onions, chopped
900g carrots, peeled and diced
1 tbsp fresh thyme leaves
1 tbsp paprika
sea salt & ground black pepper
900ml vegetable stock
juice from half a lemon
1 tbsp natural yoghurt (to serve)
fresh parsley (to serve)

Makes: 4 bowls
Prep time: 30 minutes
Cook time: 30 minutes

Method

1. Heat the oil in a large saucepan over a medium heat. Add the onions, carrots, thyme leaves and paprika. Season with plenty of salt and pepper and cook until the onions are tender (10 to 12 minutes), stirring regularly.

2. Add the vegetable stock to the pan and bring to a boil. Reduce heat and simmer, stirring occasionally, until the carrots are soft (approx. 15 minutes).

3. Use a blender to purée the mix until smooth (you will probably need to work in batches.) Transfer all to a bowl and stir in the lemon juice.

4. Serve the soup in bowls, topped with a swirl of yoghurt, a drizzle of olive oil and a little fresh parsley.

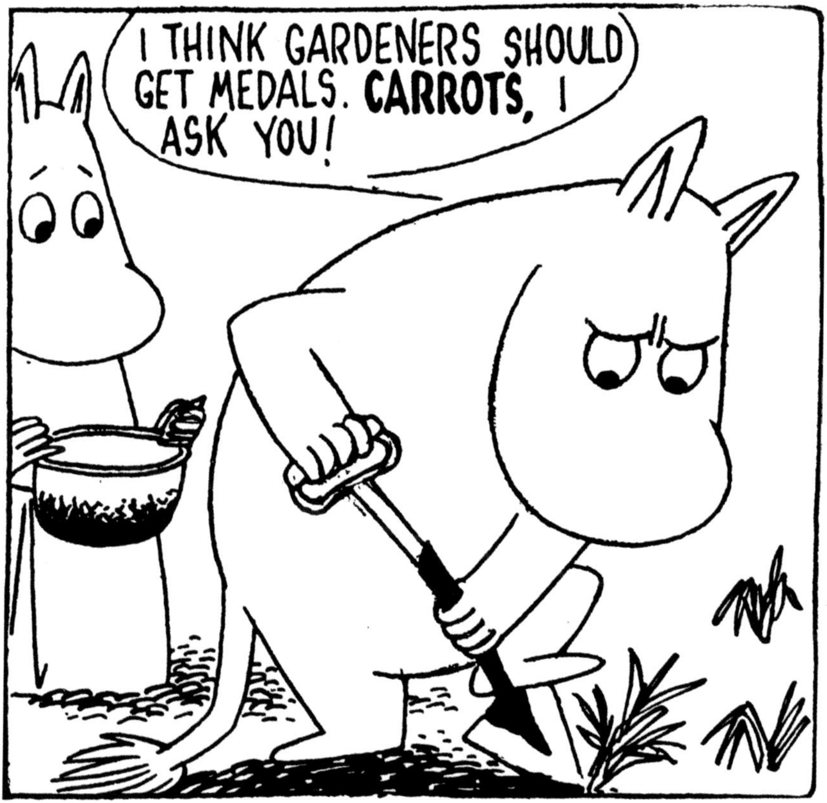
I THINK GARDENERS SHOULD GET MEDALS. **CARROTS**, I ASK YOU!

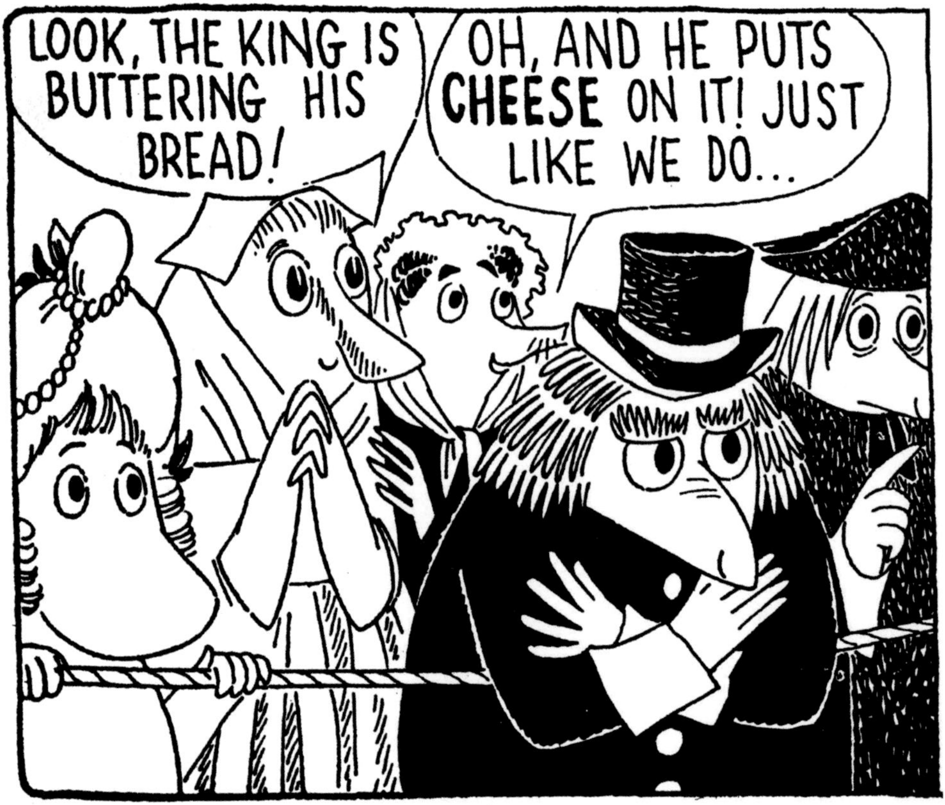
LOOK, THE KING IS BUTTERING HIS BREAD!
OH, AND HE PUTS **CHEESE** ON IT! JUST LIKE WE DO...

ROYALLY GOOD
GRILLED CHEESE

Ingredients

½ tbsp extra-virgin olive oil
1 tbsp butter
2 slices rye bread
handful baby spinach leaves
green pesto, to taste
1 avocado
100g goat's cheese, firm or semi-soft
sea salt & black pepper to season

Makes: 1 sandwich
Prep time: 10 minutes
Cook time: 5 minutes

Method

1. Heat the oil in a frying pan over a medium-high heat. While the pan is heating, butter two slices of rye bread.

2. Chop or crumble the goat's cheese into pieces and add to one slice of bread. Spread the pesto on the other piece of bread.

3. Add a layer of baby spinach leaves on top of the goat's cheese, then add slices of avocado and top with bread.

4. Place your sandwich in the heated pan. Allow to cook until the cheese has begun to melt and the underside is browned, then flip and repeat. Remove from heat, cut in half and eat like a king!

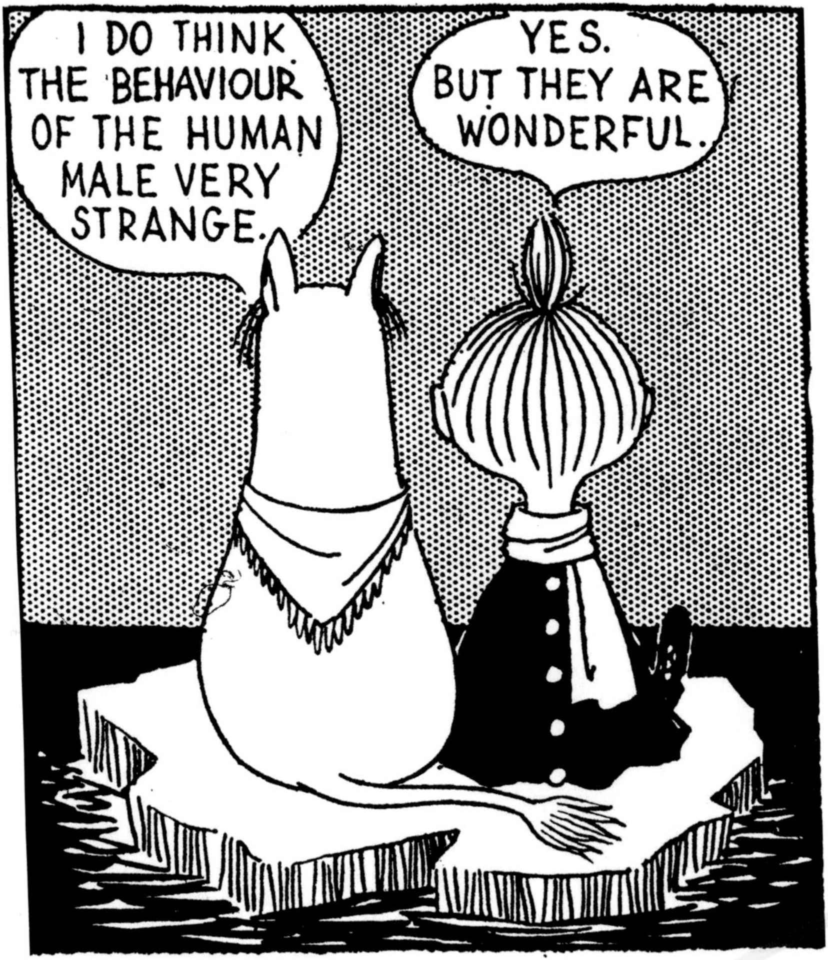
I DO THINK THE BEHAVIOUR OF THE HUMAN MALE VERY STRANGE.
YES. BUT THEY ARE WONDERFUL.

MINI MUSHROOM

MYMBLE PIES

Ingredients

115g unsalted butter
340g mushrooms (chanterelle work well)
1 large onion, finely chopped
1 carrot, finely chopped
2 cloves garlic, minced
65g plain flour
1 tbsp brandy (adults only)
590ml vegetable stock
pinch of paprika
60ml double cream
flat-leaf parsley, finely chopped
sea salt and ground black pepper, to season
1 sheet puff pastry, thawed
1 large free-range egg, lightly beaten

Makes: 4 individual pies
Prep time: 20 minutes
Cook time: 20 to 25 minutes

TURN THE PAGE FOR INSTRUCTIONS

Method

1. Place a large saucepan over a low heat and add one tablespoon of the butter. Add the mushrooms (chopped if necessary) with a pinch of salt and let them gently heat.

2. When the mushrooms have softened, turn the heat up to medium and cook them for several more minutes. Once they have caramelised, set them aside in a bowl.

3. Melt the remaining butter over a medium heat and add the chopped onion and carrot. Cook until soft (approx. 5 minutes), then add the garlic and cook for another minute, stirring regularly. Add the flour and cook for 4 minutes. Now add the brandy (if using), vegetable stock, paprika and cooked mushrooms.

4. Bring to a simmer and allow the sauce to thicken for around 4 minutes, stirring occasionally.

5. Add the double cream and stir to combine, then remove from the heat. Add the parsley and thyme, and season with salt and pepper to taste.

6. Preheat the oven to 220°C/425°F and divide the filling into four ramekins. Place them on a baking tray.

7. On a lightly floured surface, roll the puff pastry until 1cm thick. Cut four circles approximately 2cm larger than the width of the ramekins.

8. Lightly beat the egg and brush it on the rim of each ramekin and a little way down the sides. Top each pie with the puff pastry circles, gently pressing the edges over the sides of the ramekins. Brush the top of the pies with egg and (if you fancy) cut leaf shapes out of the remaining pastry and place on top.

9. Place in the oven and bake for 20 to 25 minutes, or until the tops are a lovely golden brown. Allow to cool for a few minutes before serving.

"Mymble has definitely fallen in love again."

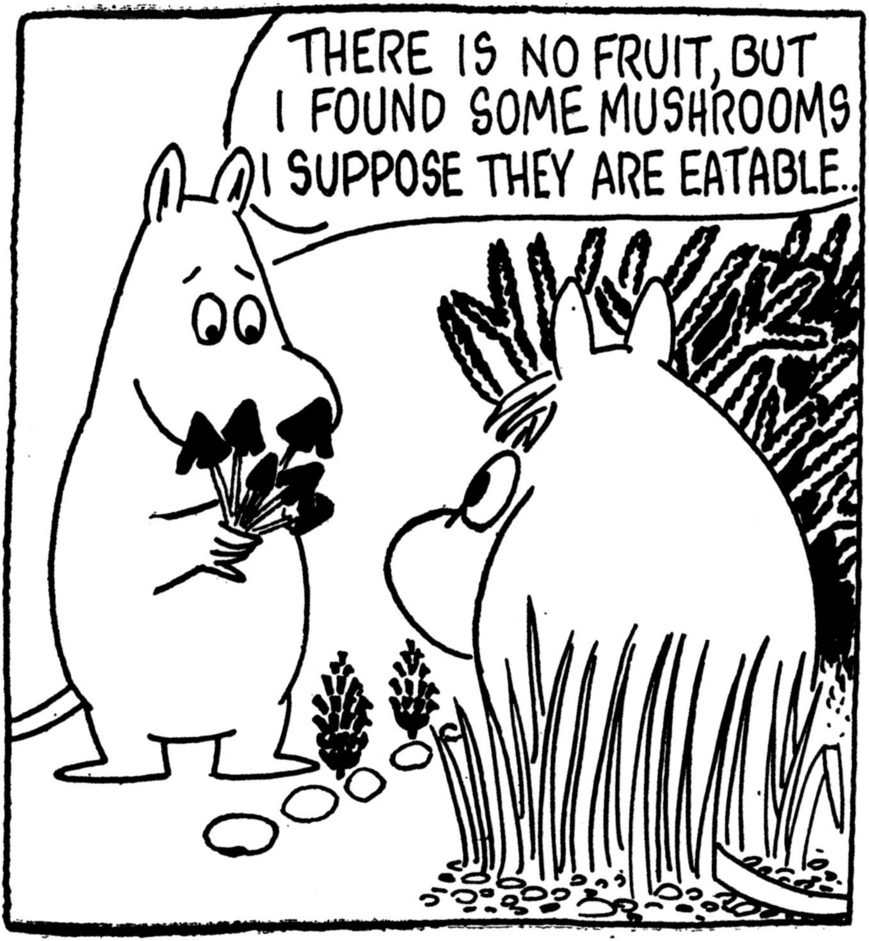
THERE IS NO FRUIT, BUT I FOUND SOME MUSHROOMS I SUPPOSE THEY ARE EATABLE..

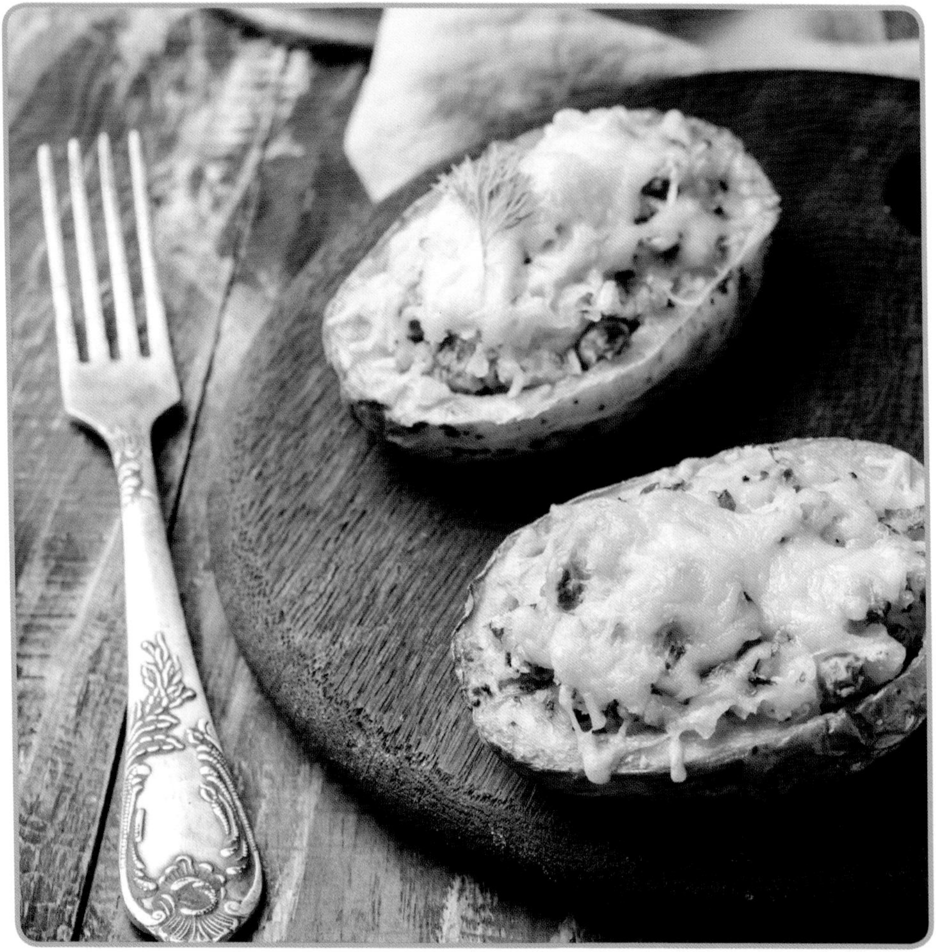

SALMON AND CHEESE
STUFFED POTATOES

Ingredients

2 medium/large potatoes
150g smoked salmon, diced
100g cream cheese
200g garden peas, frozen
3 spring onions, chopped finely
1 tbsp parsley, freshly chopped
sea salt and ground black pepper
100g cheddar cheese, grated
pinch of dill (to serve)

Makes: 4 stuffed halves
Prep time: 10 minutes
Cook time: 105 minutes

I ONLY WANT TO LIVE IN PEACE AND PLANT POTATOES AND DREAM!

Method

1. Preheat your oven to 190°C/375°F, then prick the potatoes and bake for around one and a half hours, until the skins are crispy.

2. Allow the potatoes to cool, then cut them in half lengthways and scoop out the insides. Put the insides into a separate bowl and store the skins in the fridge until you need them.

CONTINUED ON THE NEXT PAGE 23

3. Preheat the grill on a medium setting. Take the bowl of potato insides and add the cream cheese, garden peas, spring onions, parsley and salmon. Stir gently to combine. Season to taste.

4. Fetch your potato skins from the fridge and spoon your mixture into them. Add enough so they are heaped with delicious filling.

5. Top with grated cheddar cheese and extra seasoning, then place under the grill for 10 to 15 minutes, checking regularly to ensure the tops are just golden.

6. Remove your stuffed potatoes from the grill and top with dill to serve.

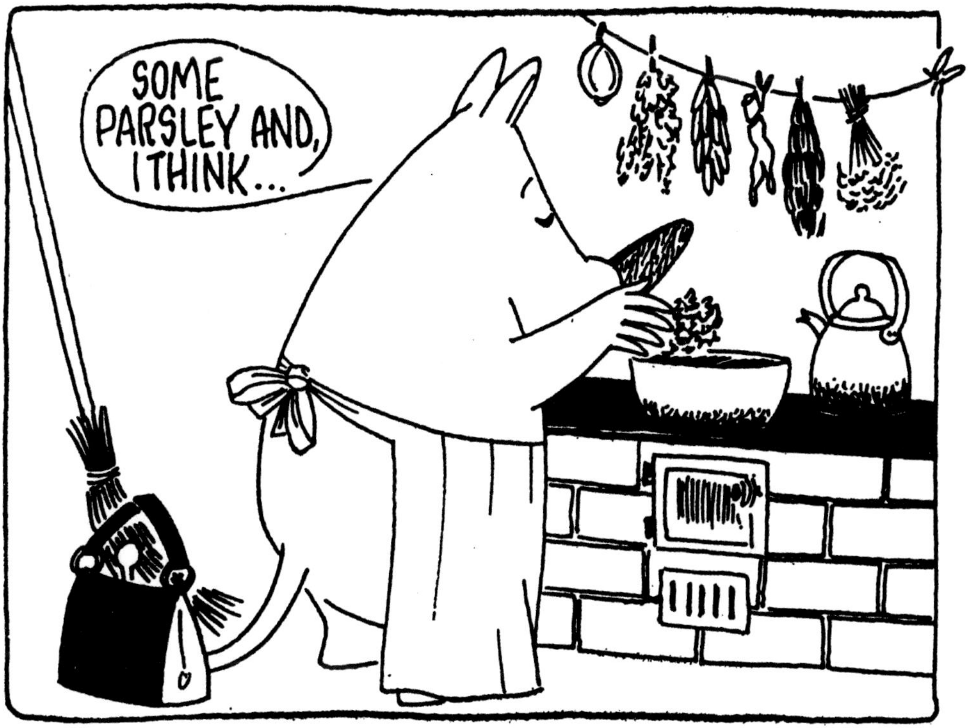
SOME PARSLEY AND, I THINK...

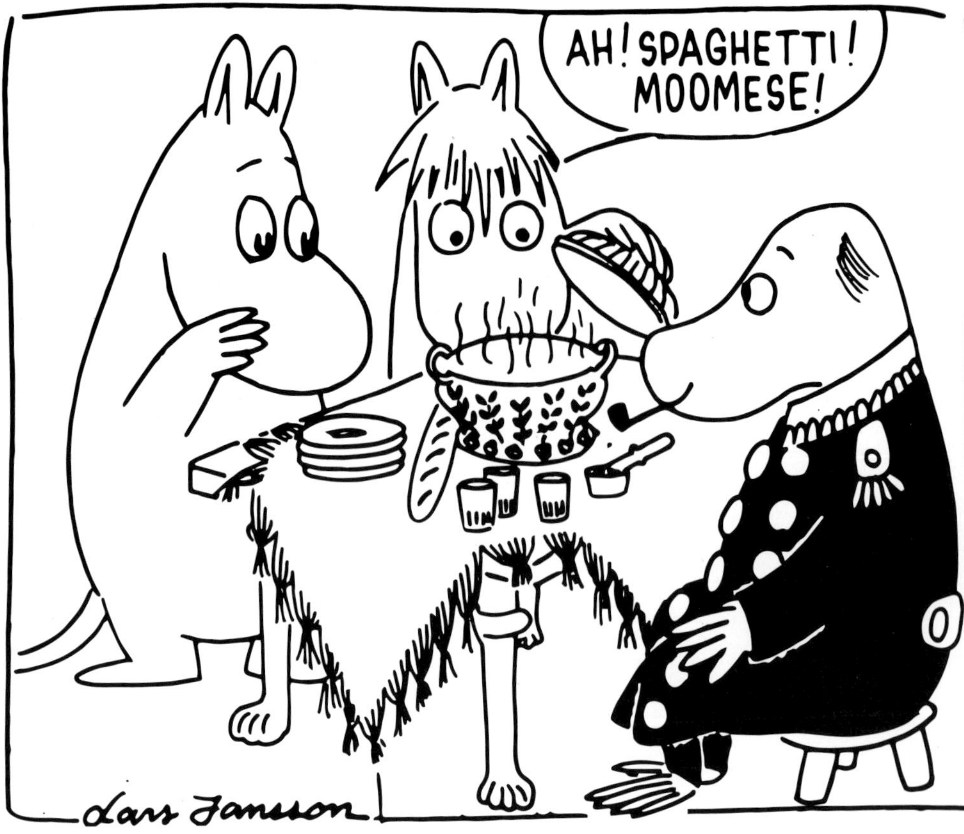
AH! SPAGHETTI!
MOOMESE!
Lars Jansson

SPAGHETTI MOOMESE

(DOES NOT CONTAIN MOOMIN)

Ingredients

175g spaghetti
1tbsp vegetable oil
1 small onion, peeled
and finely chopped
1 medium carrot, peeled and diced
1 clove garlic, finely chopped
300g vegetarian mince
150ml vegetable stock
400g can chopped tomatoes
1tbsp tomato ketchup
dash of chilli sauce
sea salt and ground black pepper
2 tbsp basil leaves, torn
grated vegetarian hard cheese
(for topping)

Serves: 4
Prep time: 10 minutes
Cook time: 40 minutes

TURN THE PAGE FOR INSTRUCTIONS

Method

1. In a large non-stick pan, heat the oil and cook the onion and diced carrot for 5 minutes, until the onion softens.

2. Add the garlic to the pan and cook for a further minute.

3. Add the vegetarian mince, stock, chopped tomatoes, ketchup and chilli sauce to the pan and stir well to combine. Season with salt and ground black pepper to taste.

4. When the mixture is just boiling, reduce the heat, cover and allow to simmer for 15 minutes – until the moisture has reduced slightly and the carrots are softened.

5. While the sauce is simmering, cook your spaghetti. Boil some water in a large pan, then add the pasta. Leave uncovered and wait for the water to return to the boil, then start timing. Use the pack as a guide, but most pastas will be ready in 8 to 12 minutes – keep testing until your spaghetti is perfectly al dente (soft but still slightly chewy). Then remove from the heat and drain using a colander.

6. Remove the sauce from the heat, then add the basil and cooked spaghetti to the pan. Stir gently to combine.

7. Transfer to four serving dishes, add grated cheese and serve immediately to warm the soul.

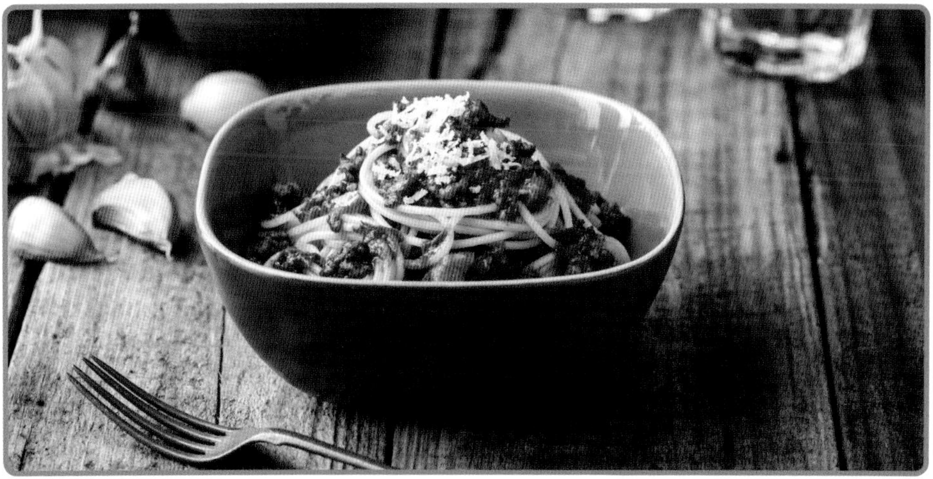

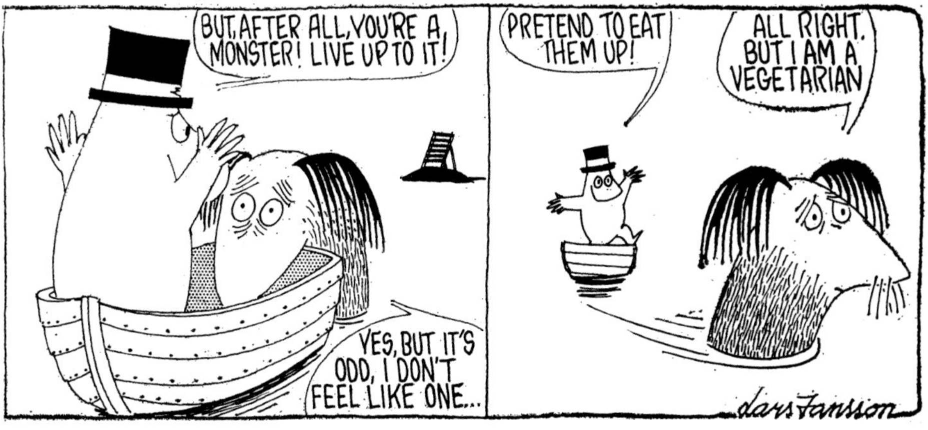

BUT, AFTER ALL, YOU'RE A MONSTER! LIVE UP TO IT!
YES, BUT IT'S ODD, I DON'T FEEL LIKE ONE...
PRETEND TO EAT THEM UP!
ALL RIGHT. BUT I AM A VEGETARIAN
Lars Jansson

LENTIL AND
SAUSAGE BAKE

Ingredients

8 sausages (meat or veggie)
1 onion, finely chopped
4 bacon rashers, finely chopped (optional)
2 garlic cloves, crushed
125ml dry white wine
400g can puy lentils, rinsed and drained
250ml stock
4 sprigs thyme
handful of spinach leaves

Makes: 4 servings
Prep time: 5 minutes
Cook time: 20 minutes

Method

1. Preheat your oven to 200°C/390°F.

2. Heat a large frying pan over a
   medium heat. Add the sausages
   and cook until brown all over
   (2 to 3 minutes). Then transfer
   them to a plate.

3. Place the chopped onion, bacon (if using)
   and garlic into the pan. Cook for 5 minutes,
   stirring regularly, until the onion softens.

4. Add the wine to the pan and cook for
   another minute, or until the mixture
   reduces by half. Remove from the heat.

5. Spoon the onion mix, along with the lentils, stock and thyme, into a casserole dish. Mix everything together and place the sausages on top. Cook in the oven for 10 minutes, or until most of the liquid is absorbed.

6. Remove from the oven and add the spinach. Gently mix until the spinach wilts just slightly from the heat of the dish. Serve immediately in warm bowls.

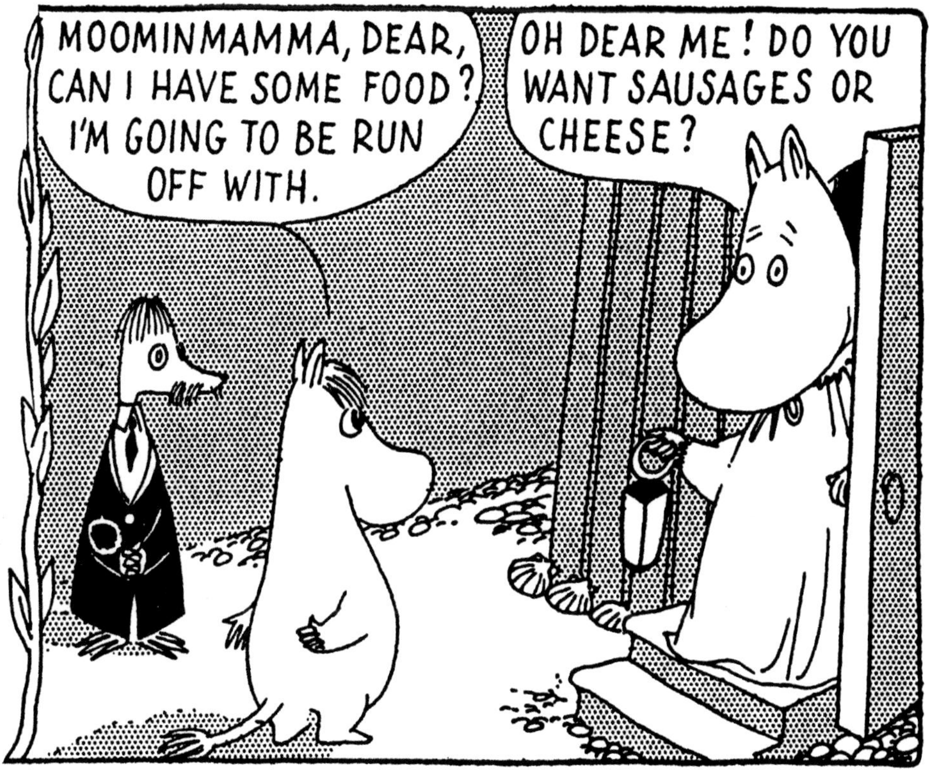
MOOMINMAMMA, DEAR, CAN I HAVE SOME FOOD? I'M GOING TO BE RUN OFF WITH.
OH DEAR ME! DO YOU WANT SAUSAGES OR CHEESE?

MOOMINTROLL'S

ROCK CAKES

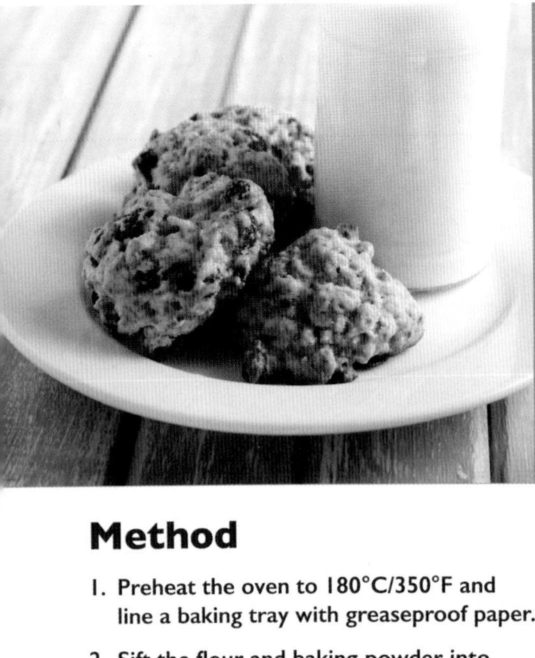

Ingredients

225g self-raising flour
75g caster sugar
1 tsp baking powder
125g unsalted butter, cut into cubes
150g sultanas
1 medium free-range egg
1 tbsp milk (or alternative)
2 tsp vanilla extract

Makes: 12 cakes approx.
Prep time: 20 minutes
Cook time: 15 to 20 minutes

Method

1. Preheat the oven to 180°C/350°F and line a baking tray with greaseproof paper.
2. Sift the flour and baking powder into a bowl, then add the sugar and mix together. Add the butter and rub the mixture with your fingers until it looks like breadcrumbs, then stir in the sultanas.
3. In a separate bowl, beat the egg, milk and vanilla extract together.
4. Add the liquid mixture to the dry ingredients and stir with a large spoon until the mixture comes together as a thick, lumpy dough. Add a teaspoon more milk if needed to form the dough.

5. Place tablespoon-sized blobs of the mixture onto the prepared baking tray, leaving space between each one, as they will expand and spread out during baking.
6. Bake for 15 to 20 minutes, until golden brown. Allow to cool for a couple of minutes on the tray, then transfer them to a wire rack to cool completely before tucking in.

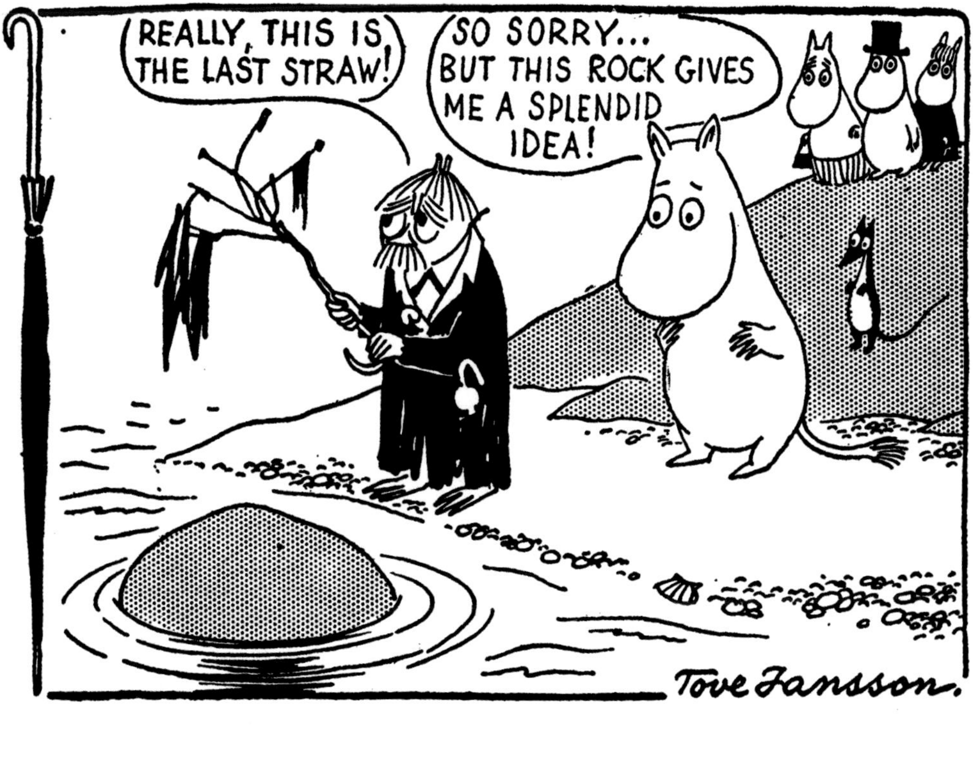
REALLY, THIS IS THE LAST STRAW!
SO SORRY... BUT THIS ROCK GIVES ME A SPLENDID IDEA!
Tove Jansson.

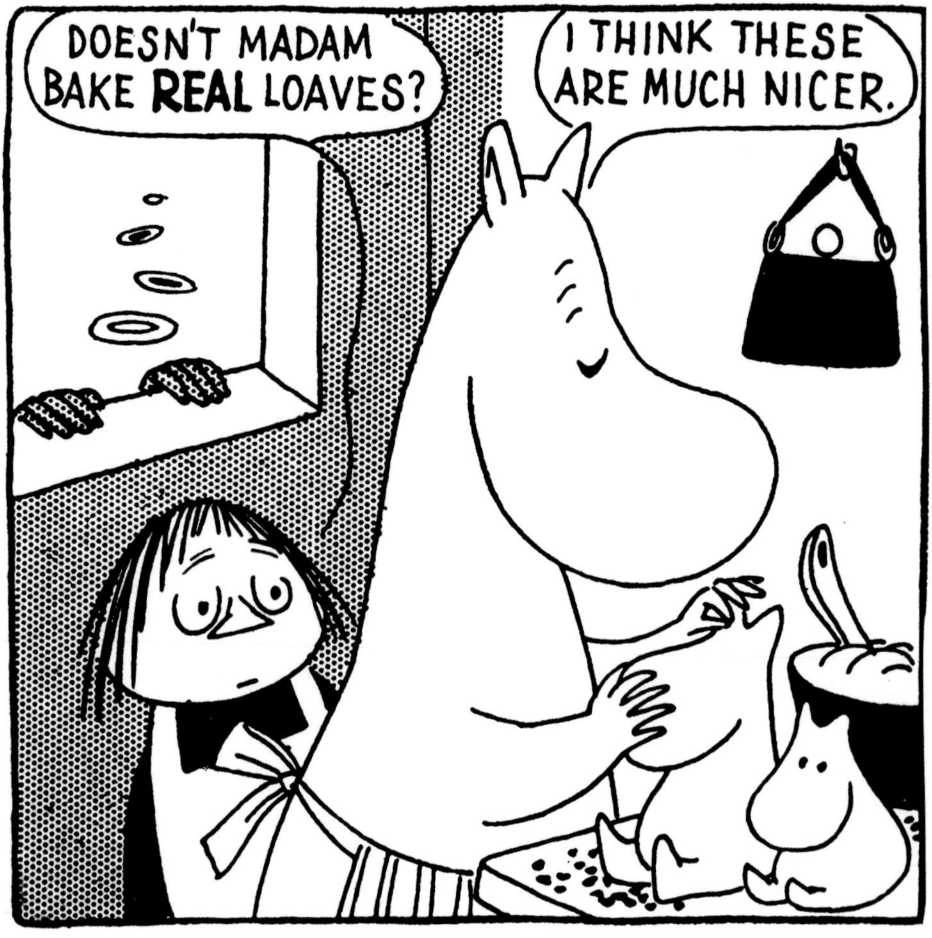
DOESN'T MADAM BAKE **REAL** LOAVES?
I THINK THESE ARE MUCH NICER.

MOOMIN-SHAPED
GINGERBREAD

Ingredients

350g plain flour, plus extra for
rolling out
1 tsp bicarbonate of soda
2 tsp ground ginger
1 tsp ground cinnamon
125g butter
175g light soft brown sugar
1 medium free-range egg
4 tbsp golden syrup

To decorate:
2 packs of white ready-to-roll
fondant icing
1 black edible icing pen

Makes: approx. 20 biscuits
Prep time: 30 minutes
Cook time: 15 minutes
Extra time: 30 minutes
(cooling and decorating)

TURN THE PAGE FOR INSTRUCTIONS

Method

1. Sift the flour, bicarbonate of soda, ginger and cinnamon and pour into a food processor bowl. Add the butter and blend until the mix looks like breadcrumbs. Now stir in the sugar.
2. In a separate bowl, lightly beat the egg and golden syrup together, then add to the food processor and pulse until the mixture clumps together.

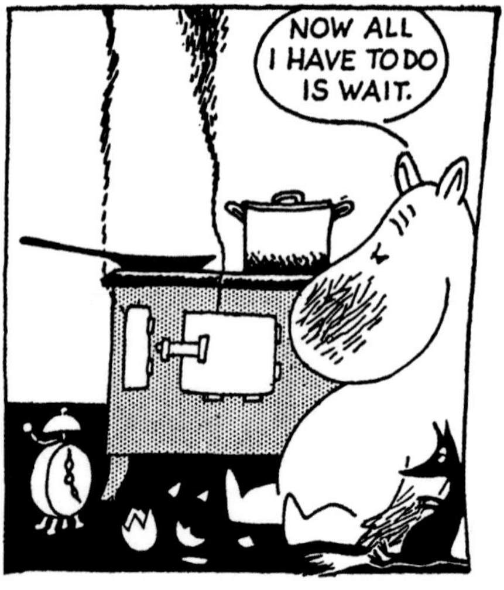
NOW ALL I HAVE TO DO IS WAIT.

3. Prepare a flat surface by dusting it with flour, then tip the dough out of the food processor bowl. Knead the dough until smooth (should only take a minute), then wrap it in cling film and place in the fridge for 15 minutes.
4. Preheat the oven to 180°C/350°F and line two baking trays with greaseproof paper.
5. Remove the dough from the fridge and, on your floured surface, roll it out until it's around 0.5cm thick.
6. Now the fun part – creating your Moomin shapes! You can do this with Moomin cookie cutters, or by hand with a knife (a blunt butter knife will do). If you're doing the latter, print out some pictures of the Moomin family and friends, cut out the shapes, place them on top of your dough and cut carefully around them.
7. Place your biscuits on the baking trays, with a good amount of space between each one (they may increase in size in the oven).

8. Bake for 12 to 15 minutes, or until lightly golden brown. Remove the trays from the oven and leave the biscuits on the trays for at least 10 minutes before moving to a wire rack to finish cooling.

9. When completely cooled, add your white fondant icing to your biscuits. Roll the fondant icing until it's around 3mm thick, then place the biscuits on top of the rolled icing and cut around them to match the shapes. Use a little water to soften the underside of the fondant icing and stick it to the biscuits.

10. Now take your black edible icing pen and get creative. Use images of the Moomin characters to carefully copy their outlines and features onto your biscuits – no need to be perfect, just keep it simple and they'll look great!

"The world is full of great and wonderful things for those who are ready for them."

LEMONY, FLOWERY
MEADOW CUPCAKES

Ingredients

115g unsalted butter, softened
115g caster sugar
2 medium free-range eggs
115g self-raising flour
2 tsp fresh squeezed lemon juice
ready rolled icing in green, white, pink
and purple (or your favourite colours)

Makes: 12 cupcakes
Prep time: 30 minutes
Cook time: 15 to 20 minutes

Method

1. Preheat the oven to 180°C/350°F and line
   a cupcake tin with cupcake cases.

2. Cream the butter and sugar together in a
   large bowl until light and fluffy. Beat in the
   eggs and sift in the flour. Add the lemon juice
   and stir until the mixture is smooth and thick.

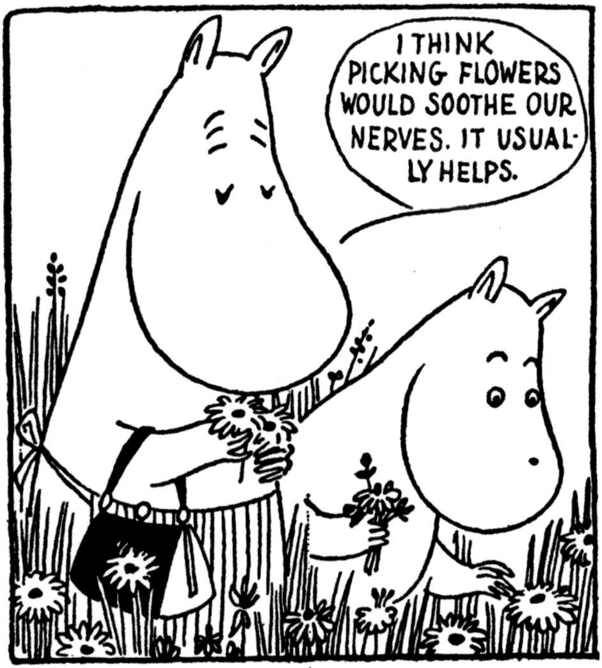
I THINK PICKING FLOWERS WOULD SOOTHE OUR NERVES. IT USUAL-LY HELPS.

"There's no need to imagine that you're a wondrous beauty, because that's what you are."

3. Divide the mixture into the 12 cases (remember they will rise, so you don't need to fill every case). Bake for 15 to 20 minutes, until they are golden brown on top and spring back when gently pressed.
4. Allow your cakes to cool in the tin for around 10 minutes before transferring to a wire rack.
5. While the cakes are cooling, prepare your icing decorations. Roll out the green icing to make a flat 'meadow' or roll pieces into tiny balls to create a textured effect. Carefully cut out flowers from your other coloured icing.
6. Once the cakes are completely cool, decorate them with your icing and share with all your friends.

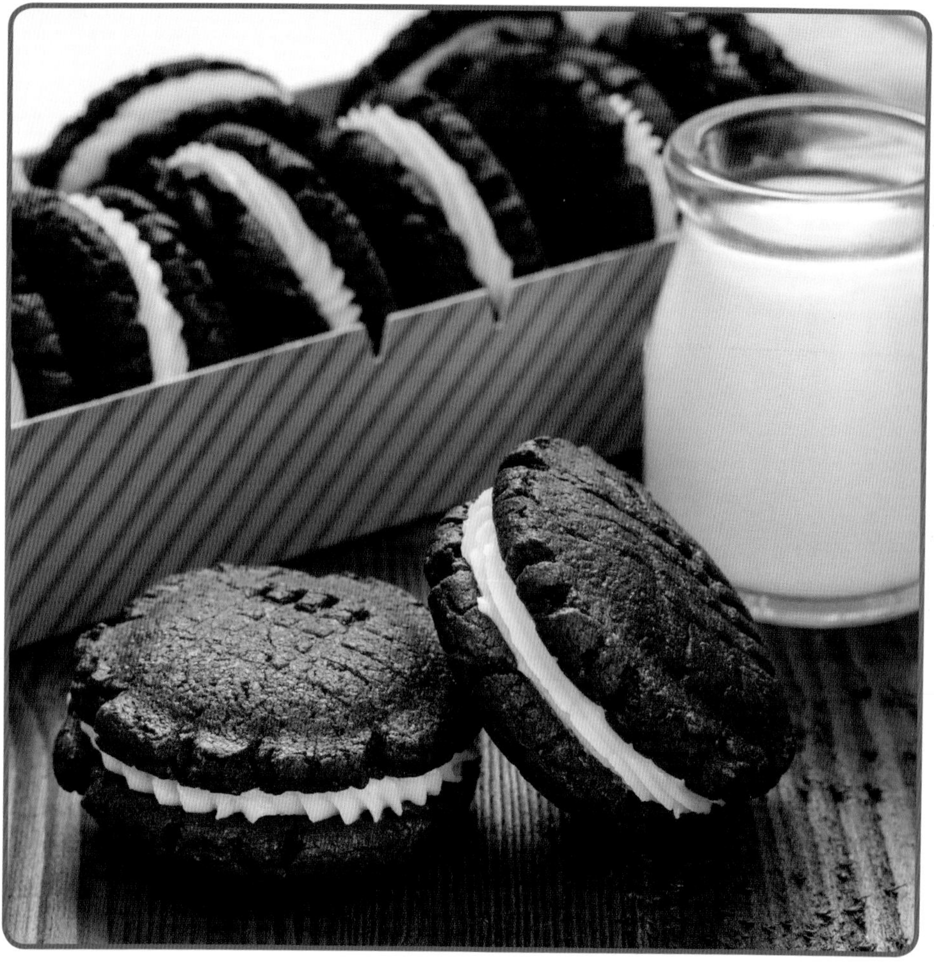

LITTLE MY'S
RED VELVETS

Ingredients

Red Velvet Cookies:
170g plain flour
2 tbsp unsweetened cocoa powder
½ tsp baking soda
½ tsp baking powder
¼ tsp salt
113g unsalted butter, room temp
100g granulated sugar
50g light brown sugar
1 large free-range egg
1 tsp pure vanilla extract
3 tsp red food colouring

Cream Cheese Filling:
110g cream cheese, room temp
57g unsalted butter, room temp
312g icing sugar
1 tsp pure vanilla extract

Makes: 20 sandwich cookies
Prep Time: 25 minutes
Cook Time: 10 minutes

Method

1. In a medium-sized bowl, sift together the flour, cocoa, baking soda, baking powder and salt. Mix until fully combined, then set aside.

2. In a separate bowl, beat together the butter and sugars until light and fluffy. Add the egg and fully combine, then beat in the vanilla and red food colouring until well mixed.

TURN THE PAGE FOR MORE

3. Slowly fold the dry ingredients into the liquid mixture. Add a small amount at a time and stir to mix fully each time. Your mixture should gradually come together into a dough.

4. Wrap the dough in cling-film and refrigerate for 20 minutes.

5. Preheat the oven to 175°C/350°F and line a baking tray with greaseproof paper. Remove the dough from the fridge and use a teaspoon to make balls of dough approximately 3cm in diameter. Place the balls on the prepared tray – leaving 5cm between them because they will flatten and spread out during baking.

6. Bake on the middle rack of the oven for 8 to 10 minutes, or until the cookies have dried on top. Do not overcook or the cookies will be too hard.

7. Leave to cool on the tray for 5 minutes, then transfer to a wire rack to cool completely.

8. Make your filling while the cookies are cooling. In a large bowl, beat the cream cheese and butter until light and fluffy.

9. Slowly sift the icing sugar into the bowl, a bit at a time, and mix until combined. Add the vanilla extract and beat until the filling is creamy and thick. Transfer to a piping bag and pipe it on to half of the cookies. (Spreading the filling with a butter knife works, too!)

10. Give each cookie a top half, then serve and enjoy!

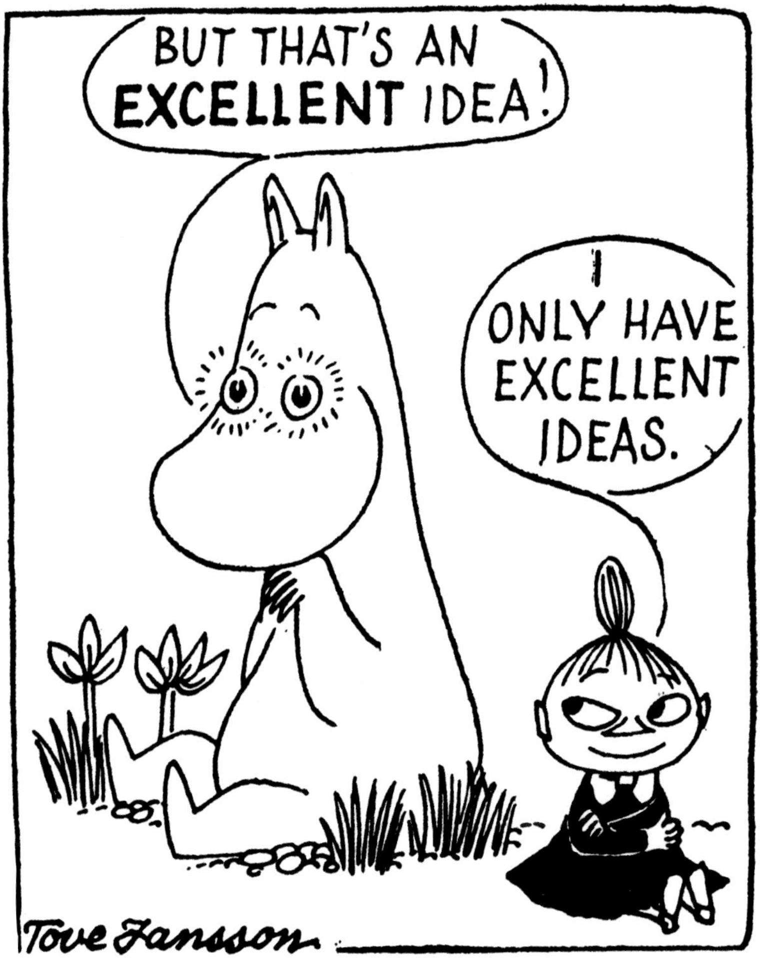
BUT THAT'S AN EXCELLENT IDEA!
I ONLY HAVE EXCELLENT IDEAS.
Tove Jansson

PEANUT BUTTER COOKIES

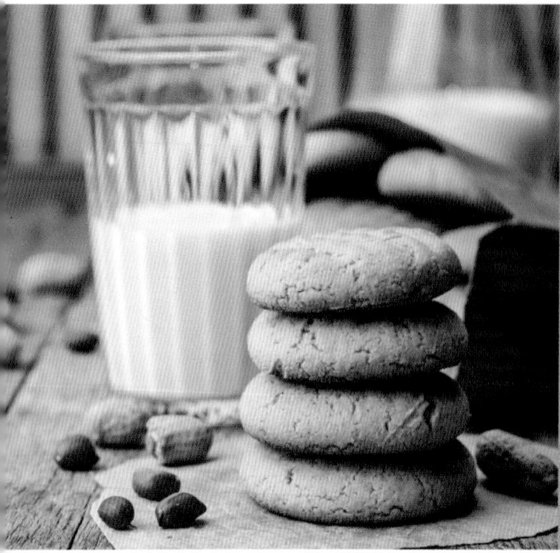

Ingredients

112g butter, room temperature
100g white granulated sugar
110g packed brown sugar
130g peanut butter
1 medium free-range egg
160g all purpose flour
¾ tsp baking soda
½ tsp baking powder
¼ tsp salt

Makes: 24 cookies
Prep time: 30 minutes (plus 3 hours to chill the dough)
Cook time: 10 minutes

Method

1. Beat the butter in a large mixing bowl until creamy, then add the brown and white sugars and beat again until blended.
2. Add the peanut butter and egg to the bowl, and mix in.
3. In a separate bowl, sift the flour, baking soda, baking powder and salt and stir until fully combined.

4. Tip the dry ingredients into the peanut-butter mixture and use your hands to bring all the ingredients together into a dough.

5. Wrap the dough in cling-film and refrigerate it for at least 3 hours.

6. Preheat the oven to 190°C/375°F and line a baking tray with grease-proof paper.

7. Unwrap the dough and shape it into 24 small balls. Place the balls about 8cm apart on your baking tray. Use a fork to flatten the balls and create a criss-cross pattern. (Tip: dip the fork in sugar first to prevent it sticking to the dough.)

8. Bake your cookies until they turn light brown – about 9 to10 minutes. (For chewier cookies, bake at 150°C/300°F for 15 minutes). Remove from the oven and allow to cool on the tray for 2 minutes.

9. Transfer the cookies to a wire rack to cool completely, then tuck in!

"All things are so very uncertain, and that's exactly what makes me feel reassured."

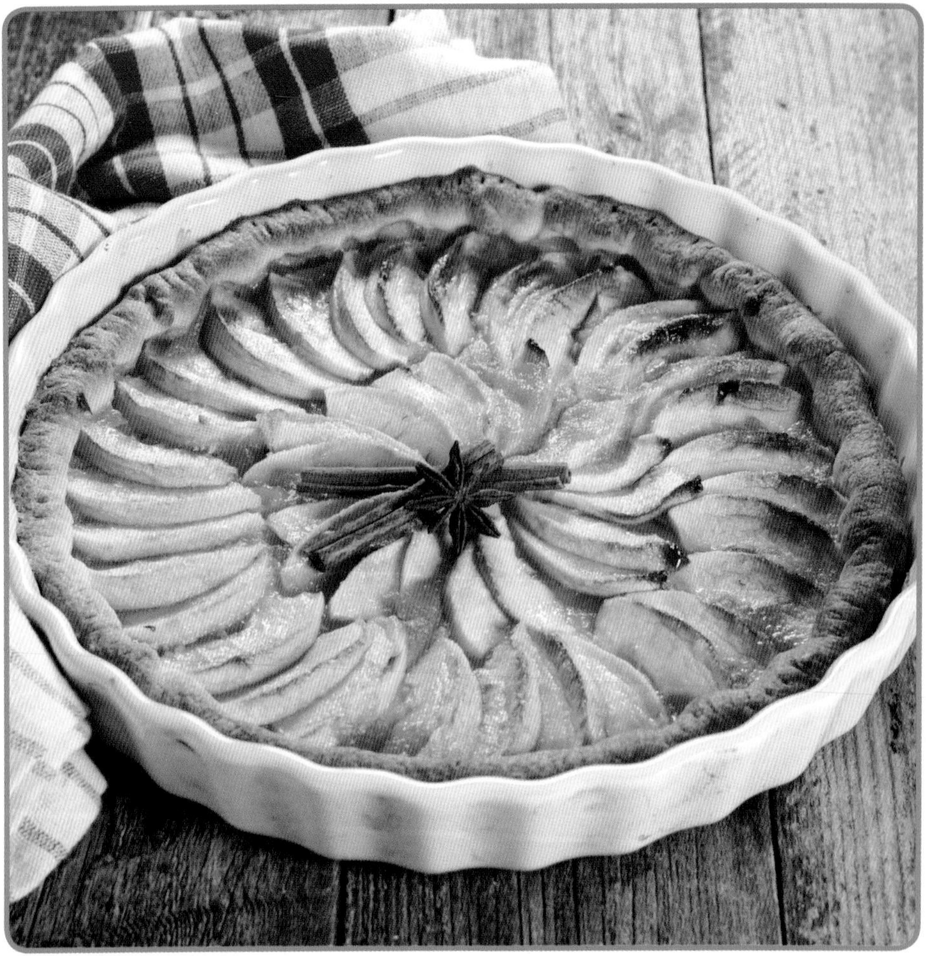

SNUFKIN'S

APPLE TART

Ingredients

For the pastry:
175g plain flour
pinch of salt
125g butter
1 egg yolk
3 tbsp cold water

For the frangipane:
125g butter, softened
100g caster sugar
1 medium free-range egg, beaten
1 egg yolk
2 tsp apple liqueur
2 tbsp plain flour
100g ground almonds
1 tsp ground cinnamon

For the filling:
3 or 4 ripe dessert apples (peeled, cored, halved and thinly sliced)
5 tbsp apricot jam
cinnamon sticks & star anise (to serve)

Makes: 1 tart
Prep time: 1 hour
Cook time: 40 minutes

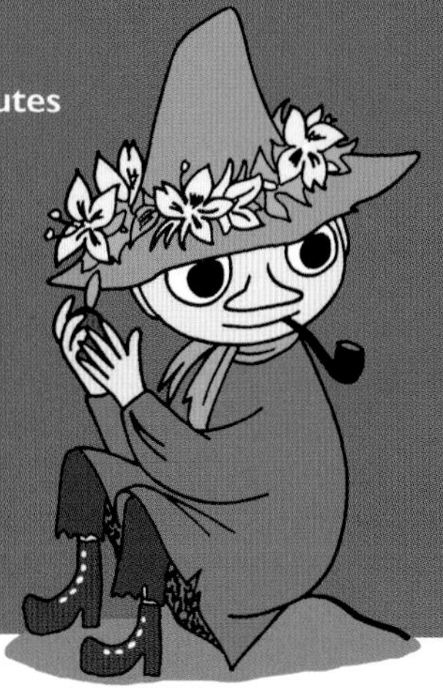

TURN THE PAGE FOR INSTRUCTIONS

Method

1. To make the pastry, stir the flour and salt together in a large bowl. Add the butter, egg yolk, salt and cold water and mix until large crumbs are formed. (If the crumbs are too dry, add a little more water.)

2. Press the crumbs firmly together to make a dough – it should be soft but not sticky. Wrap the dough in cling-film and refrigerate for at least 30 minutes, or until firm.

3. To make the frangipane, take another bowl and add the cream, butter and caster sugar. Beat until light and fluffy. Mix in the egg and extra egg yolk one at a time. Add the apple liqueur and stir well.

4. In a separate bowl, mix the flour, ground almonds and cinnamon together, then add this mixture to the batter and combine well. Set your batter aside.

5. Take your pastry dough from the fridge and, on a floured surface, roll it out into a circle large enough to cover the bottom and sides of your pie dish. Transfer to the pie dish and press into the bottom and up the sides.

6. Prick your pastry with a fork all over and flute the edges (create a crimped edge with your fingers). Place in the fridge to chill until firm.

7. Preheat a baking tray in the oven to 200°C/390°F. Take the chilled pastry from the fridge and spoon the frangipane into it, spreading it out to create an even layer.

8. Take your apple slices and create an overlapping spiral pattern on top of the frangipane. Each slice should have one edge pressed down to touch the pastry base. Start at the outside edge and work towards the centre.

9. Place the tart on the warm baking tray in the oven and bake until the frangipane begins to brown (15 to 20 minutes).

10. Now reduce the heat to 180°C/350°F and bake for another 10 minutes. Sprinkle the tart with sugar then bake for another 10 minutes (40 minutes baking in total).

11. Allow to cool completely on a wire rack. Just before serving, warm the apricot jam and brush it on top for a delicious glaze. Add cinnamon sticks and star anise to decorate (optional).

12. Serve at room temperature and enjoy!

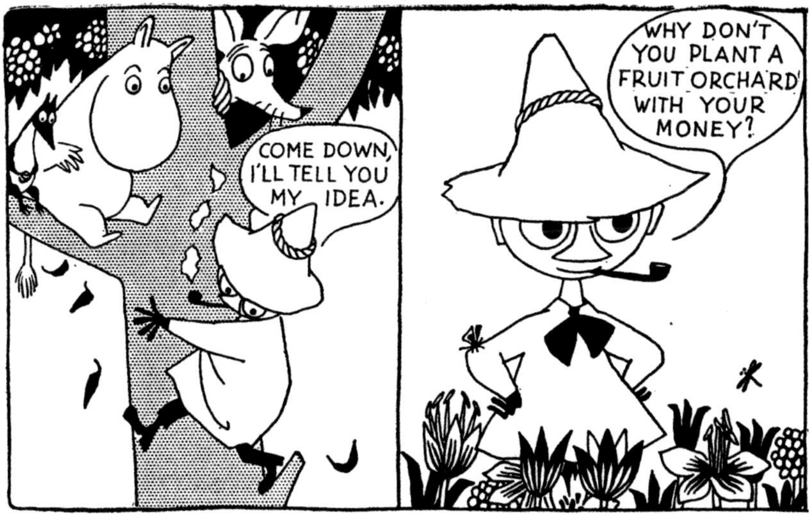
COME DOWN, I'LL TELL YOU MY IDEA.
WHY DON'T YOU PLANT A FRUIT ORCHARD WITH YOUR MONEY?

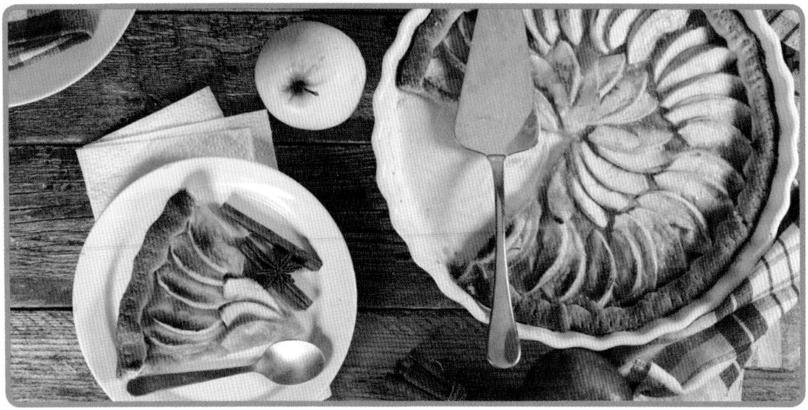

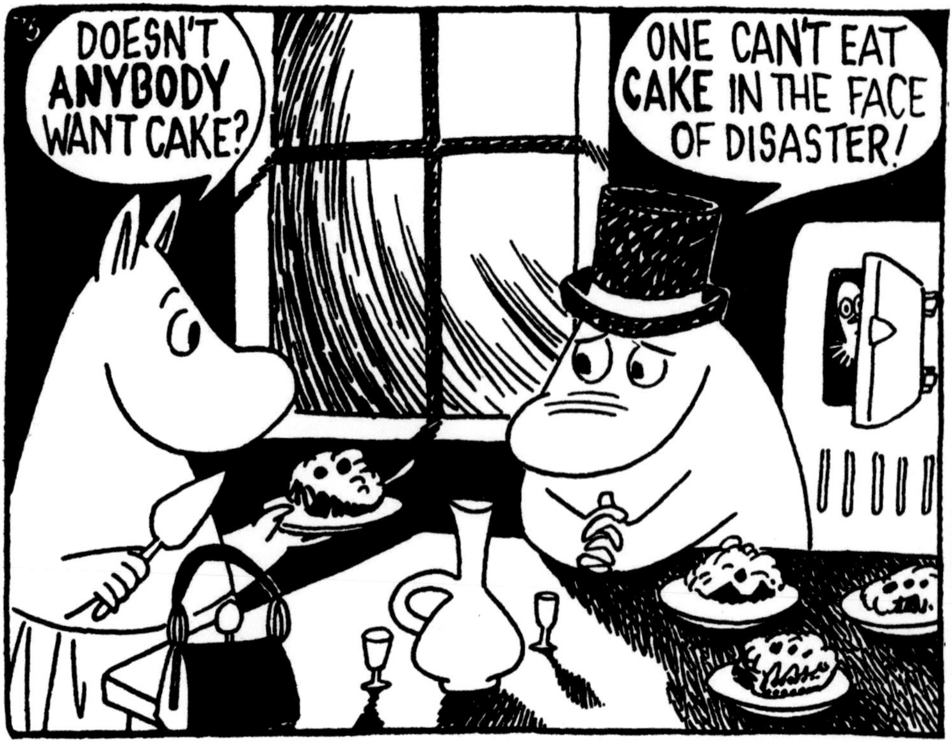
DOESN'T **ANYBODY** WANT CAKE?
ONE CAN'T EAT **CAKE** IN THE FACE OF DISASTER!

WHITE CHOCOLATE
CHEESECAKE

Ingredients

175g biscuits (shortbread or digestives)
50g unsalted butter, softened
200g white chocolate
300g cream cheese
300ml double cream
1 tsp lemon juice
1 tsp vanilla extract
handful of fresh berries (to serve)
a few mint leaves (to serve)

Makes: 1 cheesecake
Prep time: 40 minutes
Extra time: overnight to set

Method

1. First, melt the white chocolate for the topping – chop it up and place it in a heatproof bowl, then place the bowl on top of a saucepan containing 5cm of water boiling on a low heat. Make sure the base of the bowl doesn't touch the water. Once the chocolate is almost completely melted, stir it then remove from the heat and set aside to cool to room temperature – but don't let it harden.

TURN THE PAGE FOR MORE

2. To make the base, break the biscuits into a food processor and blend into crumbs. Add the butter and process again until the mixture starts to clump together. (Alternatively you can do this by hand, by putting the biscuits into a plastic bag and hitting them with something heavy, then melting the butter and stirring into the biscuit crumbs until combined.)

3. Grease and line the base of a 23cm loose-bottomed cake tin. Press the biscuit mixture into the bottom and sides of the tin with the back of a spoon. Put the tin in the fridge to chill while you make the topping.

4. For the topping, beat the cream cheese in a large bowl until it's soft. Now gently fold in the slightly cooled, melted white chocolate.

5. In a separate bowl, softly whip the double cream so it is thickened but the peaks don't hold their shape, then fold it into the white chocolate mixture in two batches. Add the lemon juice and vanilla extract and fold these in. You should end up with a pale, mousse-like mixture.

6. Pour your topping into the biscuit-lined cake tin and smooth the top. Cover your cheesecake with cling-film and store in the fridge overnight.

7. When ready to enjoy, remove from the fridge for around 10 minutes before taking out of the tin. Sprinkle delicious fresh berries on top and garnish with a few mint leaves. Voilà!

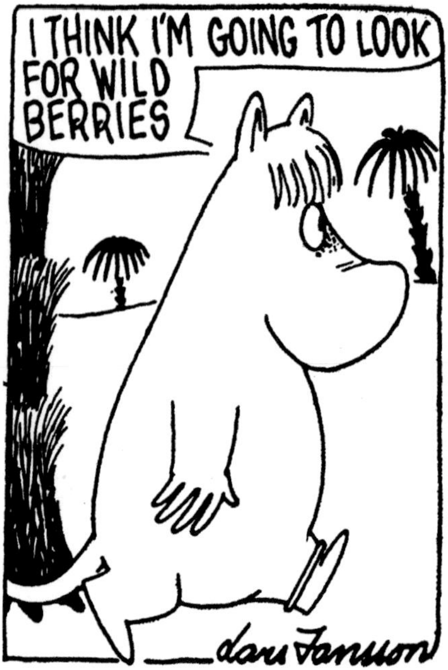
I THINK I'M GOING TO LOOK FOR WILD BERRIES
Lars Jansson

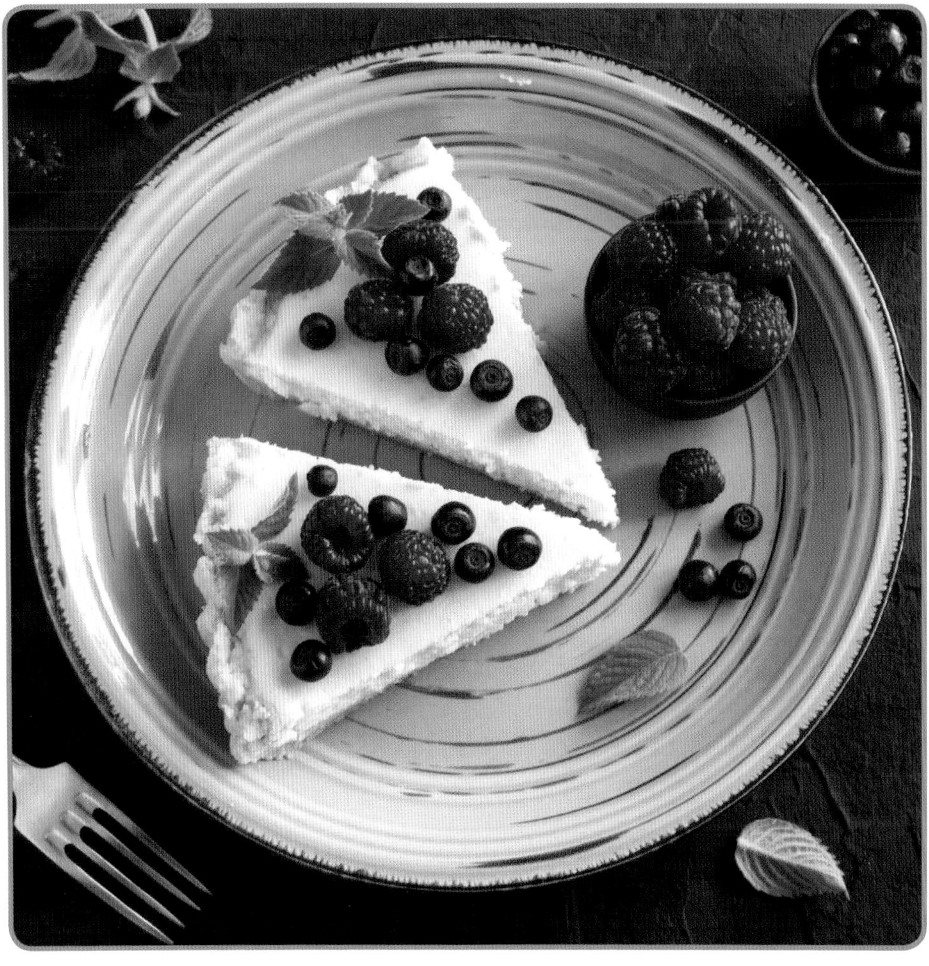

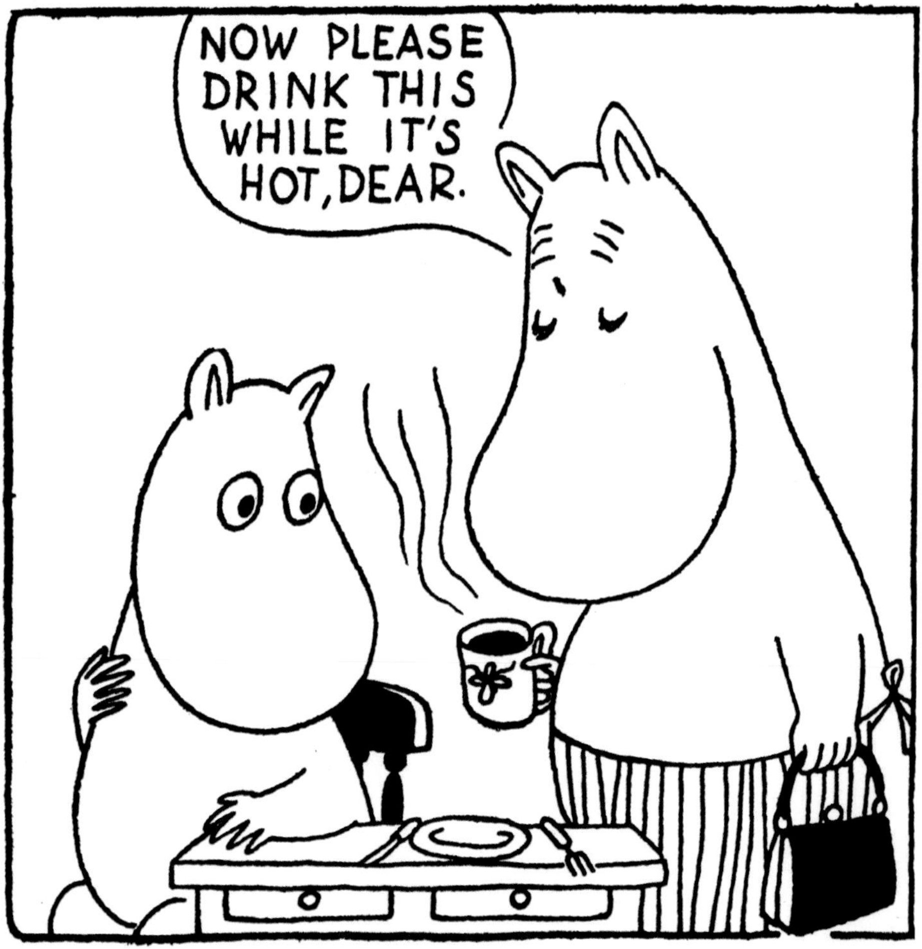
NOW PLEASE DRINK THIS WHILE IT'S HOT, DEAR.

DRINK IT WHILE IT'S
HOT CHOCOLATE

Ingredients

600ml milk
140ml double cream
100g chocolate (milk or dark)
marshmallows
extra chocolate for dusting

Makes: 4 mugs
Prep time: 2 minutes
Cook time: 5 minutes

Method

1. Chop the chocolate into small pieces and put it into a saucepan. Add the milk and double cream and heat gently, whisking constantly until the mixture is smooth. Keep the heat on low and do not allow the mixture to boil.

2. Once the chocolate has completely melted and your liquid is thick and smooth, remove from the heat. Pour your hot chocolate into individual mugs.

3. Add marshmallows and a little grated chocolate dusted over the top.

4. Enjoy at the table with your family, or curl up with your favourite book and drink it while it's hot, dear.

Oh, what happiness!

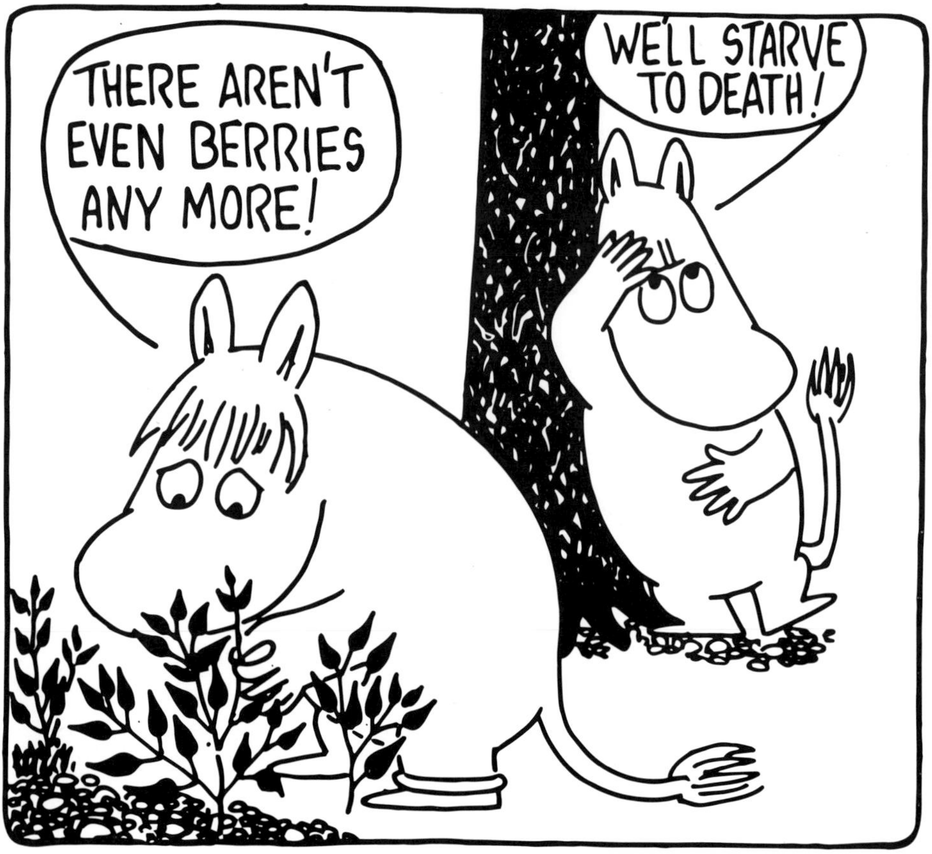
THERE AREN'T EVEN BERRIES ANY MORE!
WE'LL STARVE TO DEATH!

FOREST BERRY
SMOOTHIE

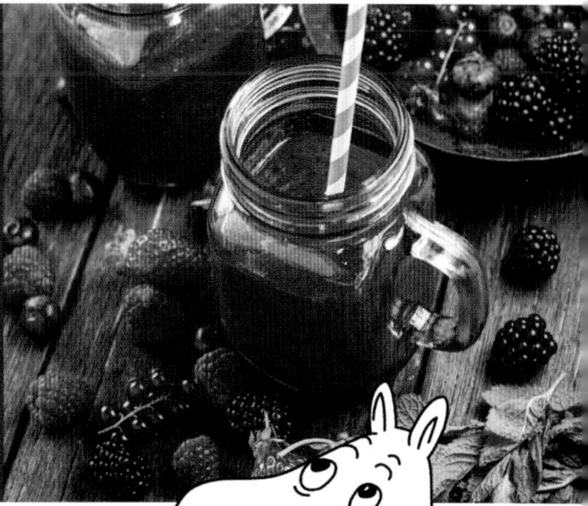

Ingredients

150g frozen forest berries
1 banana
100g of Greek or soy yoghurt
250ml milk (or alternative)
2 tbsp flour

Makes: 2 smoothies
Prep time: 2 minutes
Cook time: 5 minutes

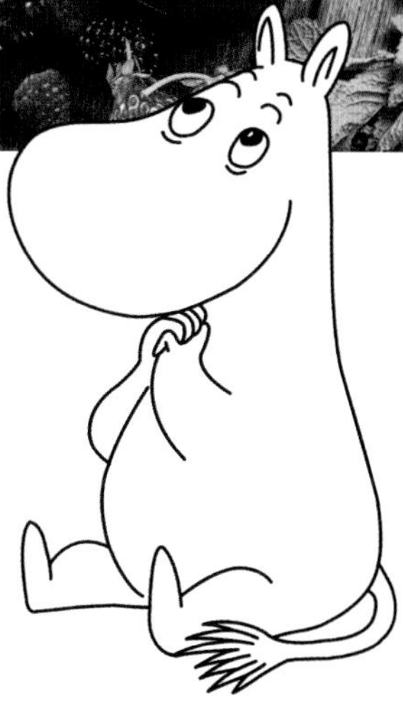

Method

1. It's really very simple ... put all ingredients into a blender and mix on high speed so that everything is completely blended and smooth. You can also use a hand blender if you don't have a regular blender at home, or if you're making smaller portions.
2. Once the mixture is smooth, pour into two tall glasses to serve. Top with extra berries, if you like!

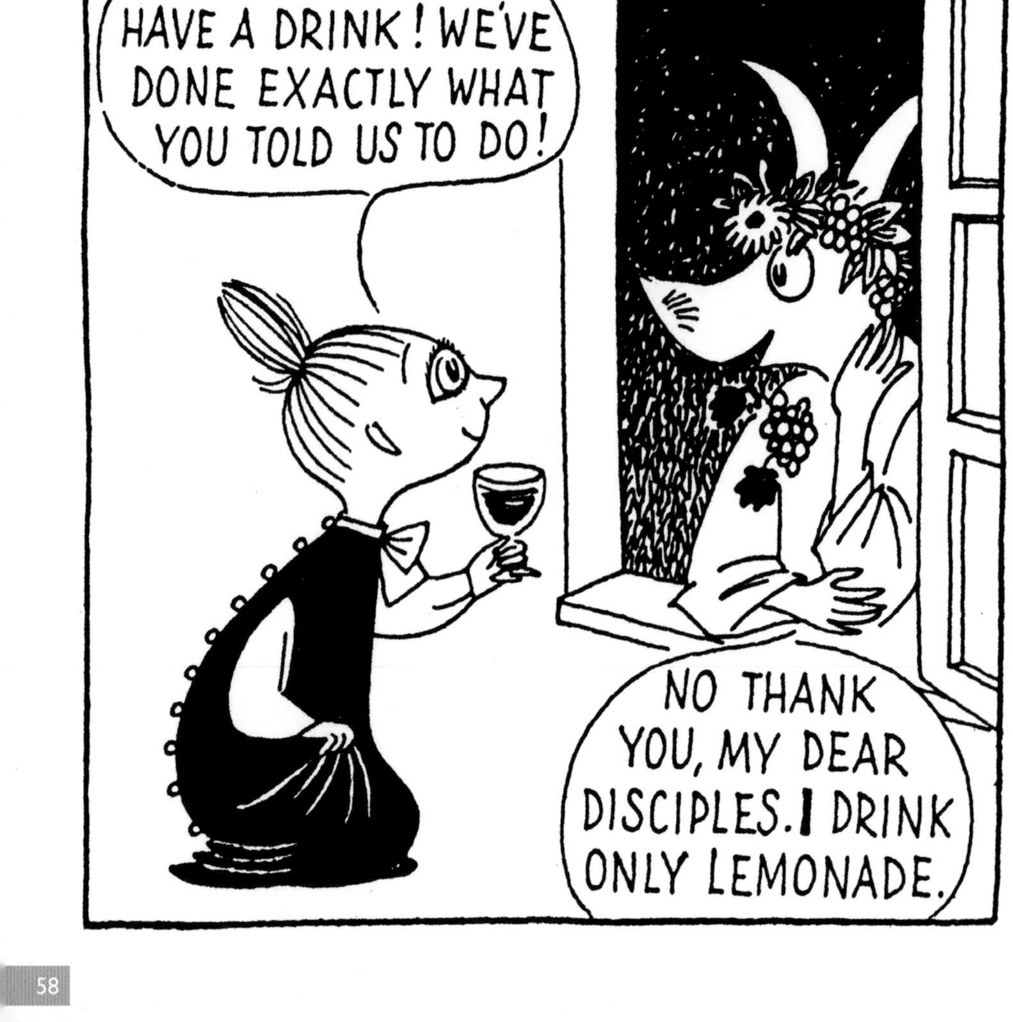
HAVE A DRINK! WE'VE DONE EXACTLY WHAT YOU TOLD US TO DO!
NO THANK YOU, MY DEAR DISCIPLES. I DRINK ONLY LEMONADE.

LUSCIOUS LEMONADE

Ingredients

180g white, granulated sugar
240ml water (for the sugar syrup)
240ml lemon juice
700ml cold water (to dilute)
ice cubes, lemon slices, mint leaves (to serve)

Makes: 6 servings
Prep time: 10 minutes

Method

1. First you'll need to make some sugar syrup. Place the sugar and 240ml water in a small saucepan and bring to a simmer. Stir regularly until the sugar dissolves completely, then remove from the heat.

2. Now juice your lemons. Four to six lemons should be enough for 240ml of juice. Cut them in half, then use a juicer or simply squeeze the juice into a bowl.

3. Combine the lemon juice and sugar syrup in a large jug. Add around 500ml of cold water and then taste your lemonade. If it's a bit too sweet, add more cold water (we recommend up to 700ml total). But note that if you're going to add ice cubes, they will dilute your lemonade, too. You can also add more lemon juice at this point if you'd like.

4. Now chill! Pop your lemonade in the fridge for at least 30 minutes.

5. Serve with ice cubes, sliced lemons and mint leaves – and enjoy with friends.

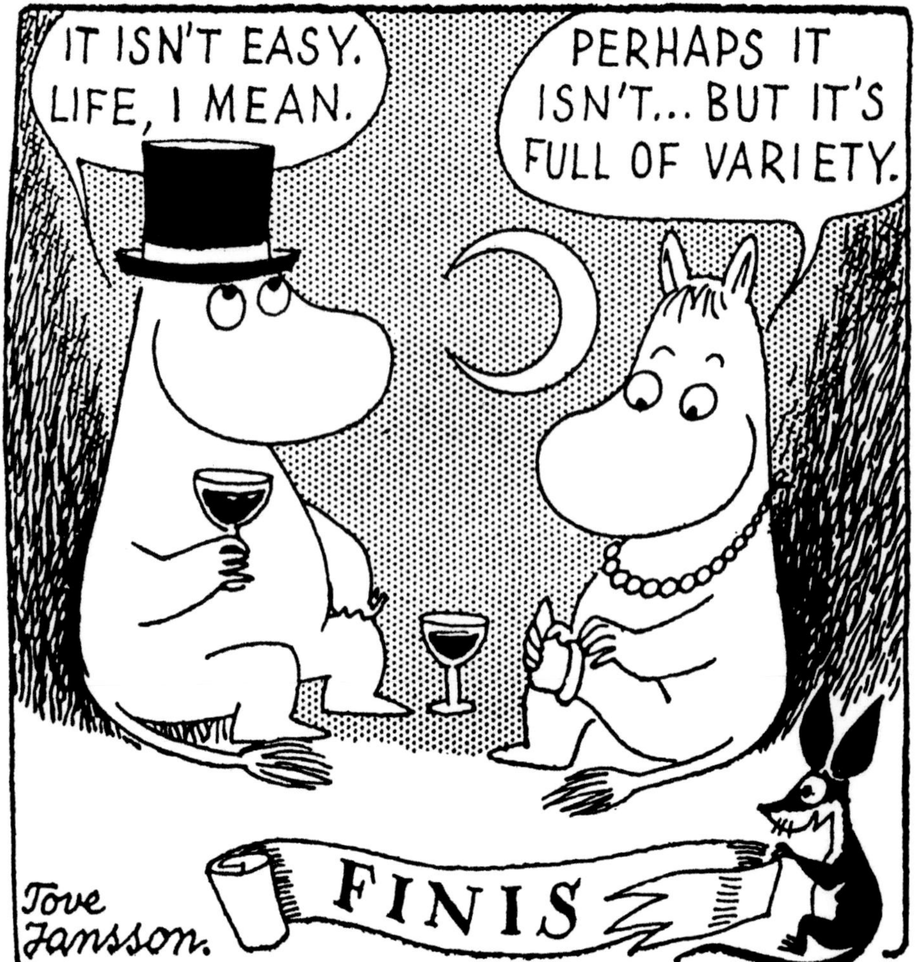
IT ISN'T EASY. LIFE, I MEAN.
PERHAPS IT ISN'T... BUT IT'S FULL OF VARIETY.
FINIS
Tove Jansson.

Photography

p9 nadianb / shutterstock.com
p10 Elena Veselova / shutterstock.com
p12 pilipphoto / shutterstock.com
p14 Anna_Pustynnikova / shutterstock.com
p17 & 44 Nataliya Arzamasova / shutterstock.com
p19 sarsmis / shutterstock.com
p22 & 24 Tanya Stolyarevskaya / shutterstock.com
p24 symbiot / shutterstock.com
p27 & 29 3523studio / shutterstock.com
p28 Hitdelight / shutterstock.com
p30 Tatiana Vorona / shutterstock.com
p32 MShev / shutterstock.com
p35 Grezova Olga / shutterstock.com
p37 Olha Afanasieva / shutterstock.com
p38 Iryna Karbovska / shutterstock.com
p40 & 42 iuliia_n / shutterstock.com
p42 Robert Gubbins / shutterstock.com
p46 & 49 margouillat photo / shutterstock.com
p51 & 53 Oksana Mizina / shutterstock.com
p55 George Dolgikh / shutterstock.com
p57 marcin jucha / shutterstock.com
p59 ESstock / shutterstock.com

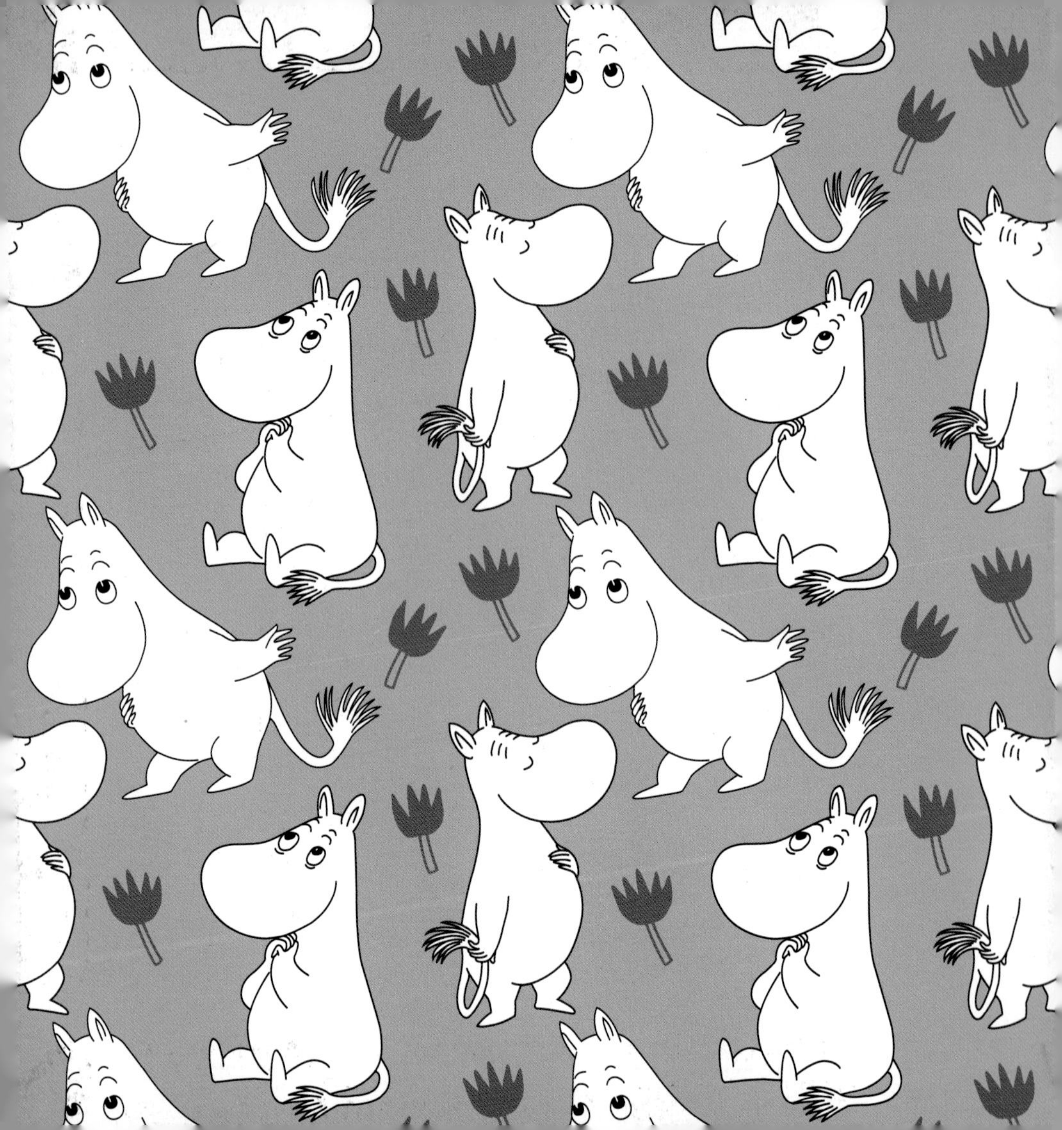